COUGAR

COUGAR

THE AMERICAN LION

by
Kevin Hansen

In Association with
The Mountain Lion Foundation

Foreword by
Robert Redford

Northland Publishing

Book Design by Larry Lindahl
Typography by Jennifer Swaffar

Manufactured in Hong Kong

For more information on mountain lions, contact:
The Mountian Lion Foundation, P.O. Box 1896,
Sacramento, California 95812.

FIRST EDITION
Second Printing, 1993
Third Printing, 1995
ISBN 0-87358-544-5

Library of Congress Catalog Card Number 92-15344
Cataloging-in-Publication Data
Hansen, Kevin
     Cougar : the American lion / by Kevin Hansen, in association with the
Mountain Lion Foundation ; foreword by Robert Redford. æ 1st ed.
     130p.   cm.
Includes bibliographical references and index.
     ISBN 0-87358-544-5 (paperback) : $19.95
     1. Pumas. 2. Wildlife conservation. I. Mountain Lion Foundation. II. Title.
QL737.C23H355 1992
599.74'428ædc20   92-15344

Photo Credits: Alan Carey, pages vi, xiv, 8, 13, 16, 20, 29, 33, 45, 54, 70, 86, 95;
Susan C. Morse, page 98; Ian C. Tait, page 49; Michael Sewell, pages 36, 62.

0583/3.5M/9-95

For Danny and Susan,
who never gave up on me

· CONTENTS ·

· FOREWORD ·

THE COUGAR WORKS A POWERFUL MAGIC on the human imagination. Perhaps it is envy. This majestic feline personifies strength, movement, grace, stealth, independence, and the wilderness spirit. It wanders enormous tracts of American wilderness at will. It is equally at home in forest, desert, jungle, or swamp. An adult cougar can bring down a full-grown mule deer in seconds. It yields to few creatures, save bears and humans.

The cougar's solitary and stealthy lifestyle feeds its mystery. Unfortunately, mystery breeds fear, myth, and misinformation. Since our European ancestors first landed on American shores 500 years ago, we have waged war on large predators. The grizzly, wolf, jaguar, and cougar are now gone from the majority of their original ranges, and loss of habitat now looms as the greatest threat to the small populations that survive. Only in the last three decades have wildlife biologists begun to chip away at the fable and folklore and reveal the cougar for the remarkable carnivore that it is.

The Mountain Lion Foundation is one organization encouraging a more enlightened view of our American lion. The Mountain Lion Foundation was instrumental in the passage of the California Wildlife Protection Act of 1990, which banned the sport hunting of cougars in California and set aside $30 million a year for the next 30 years for wildlife habitat conservation. Because of their extensive range and position high in the food chain, saving land for

cougars also protects land for other wildlife and plants.

The Mountain Lion Foundation was formed by a remarkable group of people to protect mountain lions and other wildlife. Founding leaders included one of California's leading conservationists, Margaret Owings, as well as Judge William Newsom, attorney Bill Yeates, activist Sharon Negri, and Mark J. Palmer, who all contribute time and talent to the efforts to preserve our wildlife heritage, as symbolized by the American lion roaming the last wilderness areas.

The cougar offers an unprecedented opportunity to shift our perspective of predators. This American lion has proven amazingly resilient in the face of the human onslaught. Resilient—but not invulnerable. Renowned biologist Dr. Ian McTaggart-Cowan summed up the challenge we face: "We have an opportunity to look ahead, to decide whether or not we want to share the landscape with these magnificent creatures. If we do, we must take specific steps now to bring that about." Reading *Cougar: The American Lion*, provides an excellent first step.

ROBERT REDFORD

· A C K N O W L E D G M E N T S ·

THIS BOOK WOULD NEVER HAVE BEEN POSSIBLE if Sharon Negri had not invited me to write it in the first place. Thank you, Sharon. May your new son, Tevon, grow up to see a cougar in the wild.

Mark Palmer, CEO/Conservation Director of the Mountain Lion Foundation, wielded a firm but gentle whip in keeping the book on schedule and pushing me to finish the manuscript. His discerning editorial eye improved the final book immeasurably. I also would have never survived such an undertaking without the support of my coworkers at the Mountain Lion Foundation: Carsynn Costa, Kim Klein, and Sue West. Their patience and encouragement were invaluable. Susan de Treville, Don Dianda, and Bill Yeates of the Mountain Lion Foundation's Board of Directors were kind enough to read the manuscript and to offer their comments and criticisms.

Harley Shaw and Rick Hopkins were especially gracious with their time in sharing their considerable experience and knowledge of the American lion. Their comments on the manuscript were invaluable. Their enthusiasm was infectious and I hope reflected in the pages of the book.

Sonny Bass of the South Florida Research Center planted the seeds of my interest in cougars when he allowed me to tag along on overflights of Everglades National Park, while he tracked the endangered Florida panther. He also patiently answered many questions and reviewed the manuscript.

A special thank you to Susan Morse for urging me to take a broader view of cougars, for commenting on the manuscript, for her unceasing encouragement and support, and for introducing me to the great people at Friends of the Eastern Panther: Ted Reed and Bob Rainer. The week I spent in Vermont was filled with incredible fall colors, good conversation, and a shared love of the elusive panther. May your search prove a success.

Paul Beier allowed me to follow along while he tracked lions in southern California. He reminded me how much more fun it is to be in the field than in front of a computer. It was an even greater treat to experience his sense of humor and enlightening perspective on mountain lions.

My thanks to Maurice Hornocker, Kerry Murphy, Kenney Logan, and Linda Sweanor of the Wildlife Research Institute. Maurice took the time to read and comment on the manuscript, while Kerry, Kenney and Linda demonstrated infinite patience and good humor in answering endless questions during marathon interviews.

I would like to thank and acknowledge Fred Lindzey and Wain Evans, who took time out of their busy schedules to read and critique the manuscript and to answer my questions. Bill Franklin supplied important information on Patagonia pumas, and I'm grateful. Dennis Pemble in British Columbia and Martin Jalkotsy and Ralph Schmidt in Alberta furnished valuable material on Canadian cougars. My gratitude to Dave Maehr in Florida for all the literature on panthers and for answering my questions.

Jenni Haas designed the excellent maps, figures, and tables that grace the following pages. Linnea Fronce provided the wonderful illustrations. If a picture really is worth a thousand words, I would be out of a job.

Peter Hay provided valuable insight into the publishing industry; Greg Potter offered a "nonbiologist's" perspective on an early draft of the book; and Romey Keys always listened. My gratitude to them all.

A final thank you to the many officials at federal, state, and provincial wildlife agencies throughout the United States and Canada who returned telephone calls, answered questions and filled many requests for facts and figures. You folks never get the acknowledgment you deserve for the important work you do.

Cougar: The American Lion was produced by the Mountain Lion Foundation in conjunction with Northland Publishing and made possible through the generosity of the Summerlee Foundation and Supporters of the Mountain Lion Foundation.

MY FIRST ENCOUNTER WITH A COUGAR in the wild came not in the western United States, but in southern Florida. While working as a ranger in Everglades National Park, a Florida panther crossed the road in front of my truck one night. (Panther is the common name for this elusive cat in the South.) As I braked, the big cat hesitated and, with a front paw suspended in the air, it blinked into the glare of my headlights. The light glinted in the eerie mirrors of the panther's eyes as the long tail twitched. Then the cat was gone. It glided across the pavement and melted silently into the dense sawgrass at the side of the road. I sat for a long time gazing after it into that black Florida night. The significance of this encounter may be lost on someone who lives where cougars are common, but I knew I had been granted the rare privilege of seeing the most endangered animal in Florida—and I was smitten.

A few weeks later I found myself in a small plane 300 feet over the Everglades, accompanying National Park Service biologist Sonny Bass as he tracked the endangered Florida panther. Sonny and I listened intently to the steady electronic beeps in our headphones as we gazed out the plane's windows. Somewhere below us, in the scattered tree islands that dotted the grassy prairie, were four panthers—three females and a male—each fitted with a small radio transmitter. For an hour, through endless banking turns, we isolated the signals emanating from the ground and marked the cats' locations on a map. During the entire flight I never actually saw a panther. They were never to be caught out in the open. But I knew they were there—the beeps told me so.

Radio telemetry is only one form of technology being used by scientists throughout North America to penetrate the mysterious world of the cougar. Being a solitary, stealthy, and highly mobile predator makes the big cat hard to study. Its life and habits have been subjected to in-depth research only in the last 25 years. As a result, most of what we "know" about cougars is based in fable and folklore. Thanks to the persistent and painstaking efforts of wildlife biologists, cougars are revealing themselves to be adaptable, resilient, and amazingly complex. As with any research involving a complex animal, every solved mystery presents new questions. Such is the nature of a predator whose survival depends on remaining in the shadows.

Surveying the technical literature on cougars is an equally daunting task. Not only have many books, articles, and papers been written on the subject, but a frustrating disparity exists in research methods and subsequent findings. To further complicate the matter, cougars seem to behave differently in different locations. The lack of consistent research methods makes it difficult for experts to exchange data, and the variability of cougar behavior makes the same experts reluctant to generalize.

Researcher Kenney Logan once told me that lion biologists have a saying: "Anybody can be a lion expert, and usually just about anybody is." During the many conversations I had with cougar researchers and wildlife management personnel, I was struck by the range in confidence regarding cougar biology and behavior. Those who had worked with lions for only a few years were convinced they knew what makes the big cats tick; those who had studied cougars for over ten years felt they were just beginning to scratch the surface.

We know cougars are highly territorial carnivores that appear to coexist through a sophisticated matrix of adjacent and overlapping home ranges; we know they are highly efficient predators capable of capturing a variety of prey, often much larger than themselves; we know females are attentive mothers, nurturing and training their young for up to 18 months. Unfortunately, many fundamental questions remain: no reliable way exists to count the elusive cats; no reliable method exists to determine their age; we do not know what their habitat needs are; the impacts of sport hunting on their population dynamics is poorly understood; and we don't know how many kittens survive to adulthood.

Any discussion of the cougar must eventually transcend biology and management policy and enter the moral and philosophical realm, for here lies the roots of our perspectives, and our perspectives of predators are changing. What is the value of a cougar? Do cougars possess a right to live that is equal to our perceived right to kill them? Are there things cougars can teach us? Objective science is not sufficient to answer what are fundamentally subjective questions. Consider the following: the people of California banned the sport hunting of cougars forever in 1990, and the people of Florida chose the endangered Florida panther as their state animal. Today, the rare sighting of a cougar in the wild is more likely greeted with awe and excitement than the fear and loathing of the past. Make no mistake, this shift in perspective is a force to be recognized.

Cougar: The American Lion attempts to consolidate what is and is not known about cougars in North America. My wish to keep the book small and useful to both professional and layperson, precludes making it a comprehensive treatise. Instead, I have relied upon the most recent literature available, as well as some of the best cougar experts in the country. The text presents basic natural history and behavioral information on cougars, as well as a short historical overview of the evolving relationship between cougars and humans. Both the biological and moral arguments for cougar protection are explored and a blueprint for future management is offered.

Finally, neither I nor the Mountain Lion Foundation presume to be objective about cougars, and this book reflects an advocacy bias.

THE CONSUMMATE CAT

COUGARS WERE ROAMING THE AMERICAS when humans crossed the Bering land bridge from Asia 40,000 years ago. They watched the Spanish conquer the Aztecs and the pilgrims land at Plymouth Rock. The big cats prowled the banks of the Mississippi, Colorado, and Amazon rivers. They crossed the high, windy passes of the Sierra Nevada, the Rocky Mountains, and the Andes. They witnessed the first Mormons arrive in Utah, prospectors invade the California gold fields, and gauchos herd cattle in Argentina's pampas. From the Canadian Yukon to the Straits of Magellan—over 110 degrees latitude—and from the Atlantic to the Pacific, the cougar once laid claim to the most extensive range of any land mammal in the Western Hemisphere.[1]

That cougars can be found from sea level to 14,765 feet,[2] and survive in the dense forests of the Pacific Northwest, the desert Southwest, and Florida's Everglades, is testimony to the big cat's resilience and adaptability. These qualities were put to the test as never before when European explorers set foot in the Americas in the 14th century. Early colonists viewed the lion as a threat to livestock, as a competitor for the New World's abundant game, and most importantly, as the personification of the savage and godless wilderness they meant to cleanse and civilize. Their death sentence pronounced, cougars were hunted, trapped, and shot on sight, and their habitat was stripped away as land was cleared to make way for agriculture and new towns. Today, the lion's known range in North America has been reduced to areas in the 12 western states, the Canadian provinces of British Columbia and Alberta, and a small remnant population in southern Florida. An increasing frequency of sightings suggest that some populations may still survive in parts of the eastern United States and Canada.[3]

THE CAT OF MANY NAMES

Because of their enormous range, cougars are known as "the cat of many names." Writer Claude T. Barnes listed 18 native South American, and 25 native North American, and 40 English names.[4] The cougar is listed in dictionaries under more names than any other animal in the world.[5] The Guarani Indians of Brazil called them *cuguacuarana*, which French naturalist Georges Buffon corrupted into *cougar*.[6,7] *Puma* comes from Quichua, an Inca language, meaning "a powerful animal."[6,8] To the Cherokee of the southeastern United States the big cat was *Klandagi*, "Lord of the Forest," while the Chickasaws called him *Koe-Ishto*, or *Ko-Icto*, the "Cat of God."[7] In Mexico they are *leopardo*, to other Spanish-Americans, *el léon*.[6,7]

In 1500, Amerigo Vespucci was the first white man to sight and record a cougar in the Western Hemisphere. Vespucci, after whom the two American continents are

near the Florida Everglades.[8]

Tyger was another name used for the American lion throughout the Carolinas, Georgia, and Florida during the 15th and 16th centuries.[7] Today, cougar, mountain lion, and puma are the most common names used in the western United States, while panther, painter, and catamount are

HISTORICAL AND CURRENT RANGE OF THE COUGAR IN THE WESTERN HEMISPHERE
(Status of Cougar in Mexico, Central, and South America is unknown.)

HISTORICAL RANGE

CURRENT RANGE

Sources: Young and Goldman 1946, Dixon 1982, Anderson 1983, Lindzey 1987, Hummel 1990, Sunquist 1991.

named, was probing the coastline of Nicaragua when he saw what he described to be lions, probably because of their similarity to the more familiar African lion.[8,9] Two years later, on his fourth voyage to the New World, Christopher Columbus saw "lions" along the beaches of what are now Honduras and Nicaragua.[6,7,8] The honor of being the first European to sight a "lion" in North America fell to Alvar Nuñez Cabeza de Vaca, who in 1513, saw one

more frequently heard east of the Mississippi. Panther is the Greek word for leopard; painter is an American colloquial term for panther; and catamount is a New England expression, meaning "cat-of-the-mountains."[10] Biologists call it *Felis concolor*, literally, "cat of one color." Throughout this book, the names cougar, mountain lion, puma, and panther are used interchangeably.

FROM WHENCE CAME CATS?

The fossil record of felines is as filled with mystery as today's cats themselves. Paleontologists and biologists have traditionally relied upon fossils and differences in physical structure of modern animals to map the evolution of a particular species. This has proven difficult with cats for two reasons: most ancestral cats occupied tropical forests, where the conditions for the preservation of fossils is poor; and most of the physical characteristics of cats are related to the capture of prey, with the result that all felines are very similar in structure.[11] As a result, no less than five different hypotheses have been offered to explain the relationships between the various groups and subgroups of extinct and modern cats.[12]

While there are differing interpretations of the evolution of the cat family (Felidae), a few facts are agreed upon. Modern and extinct carnivores had a common ancestor called *miacids*. These primitive, tree-dwelling carnivores lived in the forests of the Northern Hemisphere 39 to 60 million years ago. Then, about 40 million years ago, a burst of evolution and diversification produced the modern families of carnivores. These new carnivores fall into two major groups: a bear-like group (*arctoids*), consisting of modern bears, seals, dogs, raccoons, pandas, badgers, skunks, weasels, and their relatives; and a cat-like group (*aeluroids*), a lineage including the cats, hyenas (yes, that's right), genets, civets, and mongooses.[12]

The first cat-like carnivores to appear were the saber-tooth cats, about 35 million years ago.[11] The sabertooths became extinct about 10,000 years ago worldwide, at the end of the last glaciation.[13] While the sabertooths met their demise, however, the modern cats were evolving and diversifying. Ancestral pumas lived in North America from three to one million years ago, with modern pumas appearing about 100,000 years ago or less.[11] The American lion had arrived.

THE FAMILY OF CATS

Just as there is disagreement about where cats came from, there is debate over how to classify the 37 species of cats that exist today. I discovered no less than six different proposed classification systems for Felidae during the research for this book. The Latin name *Felis concolor* was first given to the cougar in 1771 by Carolus Linneaus, the father of taxonomy. (It was Linneaus who devised the binomial system for describing and classifying plants and animals.)[8]

Today, scientists generally divide the cat family (Felidae) into two groups, or genera: *Panthera*, the large roaring cats, and *Felis*, the smaller purring cats.[11] The ability to roar depends on the structure of the hyoid bone, to which the muscles of the trachea (windpipe) and larynx (voicebox) are attached. The tiger (*Panthera tigris*), African lion (*Panthera leo*),

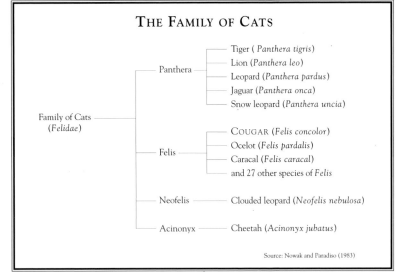

THE FAMILY OF CATS

Family of Cats (*Felidae*)

- Panthera
  - Tiger (*Panthera tigris*)
  - Lion (*Panthera leo*)
  - Leopard (*Panthera pardus*)
  - Jaguar (*Panthera onca*)
  - Snow leopard (*Panthera uncia*)
- Felis
  - COUGAR (*Felis concolor*)
  - Ocelot (*Felis pardalis*)
  - Caracal (*Felis caracal*)
  - and 27 other species of *Felis*
- Neofelis
  - Clouded leopard (*Neofelis nebulosa*)
- Acinonyx
  - Cheetah (*Acinonyx jubatus*)

Source: Nowak and Paradiso (1983)

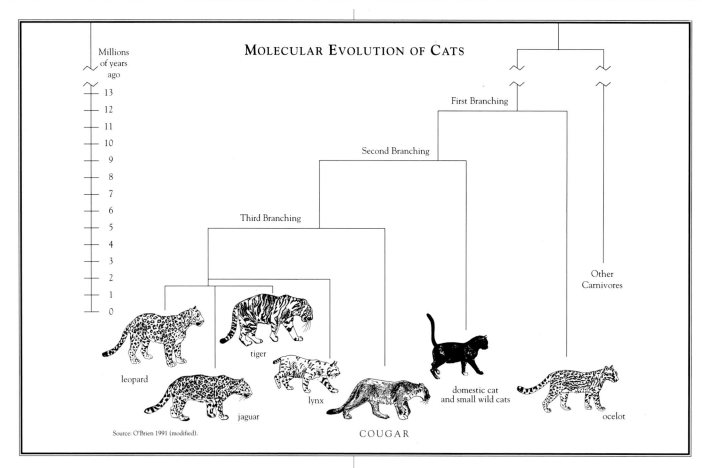

MOLECULAR EVOLUTION OF CATS

Millions of years ago

13
12
11
10
9
8
7
6
5
4
3
2
1
0

First Branching

Second Branching

Third Branching

Other Carnivores

leopard

jaguar

tiger

lynx

domestic cat
and small wild cats

ocelot

COUGAR

Source: O'Brien 1991 (modified).

leopard (*Panthera pardus*), and jaguar (*Panthera onca*) represent this group. Members of *Felis* possess the ability to purr or make shrill, higher-pitched sounds. Of the seven cat species in North America, only the jaguar (*Panther onca*) belongs to Panthera. The other six—cougar (*Felis concolor*), lynx (*Lynx canadensis*), bobcat (*Lynx rufus*), margay (*Felis wiedii*), ocelot (*Felis pardalis*), and jaguarundi (*Felis yagouaroundi*)—are purring cats and are members of *Felis*.[14] The cougar is the largest of the purring cats.

A different approach to the evolutionary and taxonomic puzzle of feline classification was taken recently through the application of the new science of molecular evolution. By examining the rate of change of the genes in the DNA molecules of different cat species, biologist Stephen J. O'Brien and his colleagues revealed that the 37 species of modern cats evolved in three distinct lines. The earliest branch occurred 12 million years ago and includes the seven species of small South American cats (ocelot, jaguarundi, and others). The second branching took place 8 to 20 million years ago and included the domestic cat and five close relatives (Pallas's cat, sand cat, and others). About 4 to 6 million years ago a third branch split and gave rise to the middle-sized and large cats. The most recent split (1.8 to 3.8 million years ago) divided the lynxes and the large cats. This third line gave rise to 24 of the 37 species of living cats, including the cougar, cheetah, and all big cats.[15]

The differences of these two classification systems are apparent and are representative of the disagreement among experts. Some biologists believe we have progressed as far as we can in our understanding of feline taxonomy through the examination of museum specimens, and that future answers lie in the study of behavior, ecology, and genetics.[16] For instance, a cheetah-like cat existed in North America less than a million years ago, but was extinct by the end of the Pleistocene era (10,000 years ago). It evolved in parallel with the modern African cheetah (*Acinonyx jubatus*) and was similar in appearance; however, it appears to have been more closely related to the living cougar than to the cheetah.[11,13] Resolving where cougars fit into the cat family would give us one more piece of the puzzle of how the American lion came to be.

SUBSPECIES AND STATUS

When a species is as broadly distributed as the cougar, regional variations in physical appearance occur. For instance, mountain lions from Alberta look somewhat different than the Florida panther, a fact that relates to the different geographic habitats in which the lion lives.[17] Wildlife taxonomists recognize these regional variations by dividing *Felis concolor* into some 26 subspecies or geographic races, scattered across North and South America.[18] This is similar to the different races or breeds of the domestic dog. Edward A. Goldman, coauthor of the classic, *The Puma: Mysterious American Cat*, explains how the subspecies of cougar are classified: "The subspecies or geographic races of the puma, like those of other animals, are

based on combinations of characters, including size, color, and details of cranial [skull] and dental structure...."[6] Twelve subspecies are recognized north of the border between the United States and Mexico.[6,7,18] (When writing the scientific name of a particular subspecies, such as the cougar found in Colorado, the subspecies name follows the genus and species. Thus, the Colorado cougar becomes *Felis concolor hippolestes* or *F. c. hippolestes*.)

The existence and status of the various subspecies of cougars in North America is the subject of heated debate among academics and wildlife professionals. The two subspecies found in eastern North America, the eastern panther (*Felis concolor couguar*) and the Florida panther (*F. c. coryi*), are classified as endangered and fully protected.[19] The Yuma puma (*F. c. browni*), a subspecies found along the lower Colorado River, is currently a candidate for listing as endangered.[20] While cougar populations are considered to be healthy in many parts of western North America, populations adjacent to rapidly expanding urban areas are facing critical habitat loss. In southern California for example, mountain lions in the Santa Monica Mountains and Santa Ana Mountains are fast losing ground to rampant residential development. Chapter 6 will discuss the status of mountain lions in North America in more detail.

APPEARANCE AND SIZE

The cougar is plain-colored like the African lion, but is of slighter build with a head that is smaller in proportion to its body. Male pumas do not have the distinctive mane and tufted tail of their Old World cousins.[2] The absence of a mane led to an early myth about mountain lions: Early Dutch traders in New York were puzzled that the lion skins they obtained were those of females only. They questioned Indian hunters and were assured that such animals existed, but only in the most inaccessible mountainous places, where it would be foolhardy to attempt to hunt them.[1]

Except for the smaller jaguarundi of Central and South America, the cougar is the only plain-colored cat in the Americas.[2] The sides of the muzzle and the backs of the ears are dark brown or black, while the chin, upper lip, chest, and belly are creamy white.[21] Atop the small head sit a pair of short, rounded ears. The cougar's long and heavy tail is perhaps its most distinctive feature. Measuring almost two-thirds the length of the head and body, it is tipped with brown and black.

Cougars are the largest native North American cat except for the slightly larger jaguar (*Panthera onca*), which is occasionally found in the southwestern United States.[22] The sexes look alike, though males are 30 to 40 percent larger than females.[23] The largest animals are found in the northern and southern extremes of its range. Though sizes vary greatly throughout the cat's geographical range, a typical adult male will weigh 110 to

180 pounds and the female 80 to 130 pounds. Exceptional individuals have exceeded 200 pounds, but this is rare. Males will measure 6 to 8 feet from nose to tail tip and females 5 to 7 feet.[2]

In captivity, cougars have lived as long as 21 years.[24] In the wild, the cats probably live only half as long. Lack of a reliable way to determine a mountain lion's age makes exact measurements difficult. In the wild, a 10-year-old lion is likely a very old cat. Experts also disagree over which gender lives longer on the average. Some think the added stress of raising kittens guarantees female lions a shorter life. The lifespan of both sexes in hunted populations is probably shorter.[25] But, even in the absence of hunting, a short life span is to be expected of a predator that faces the frequent hazards of feeding on prey much larger than itself.

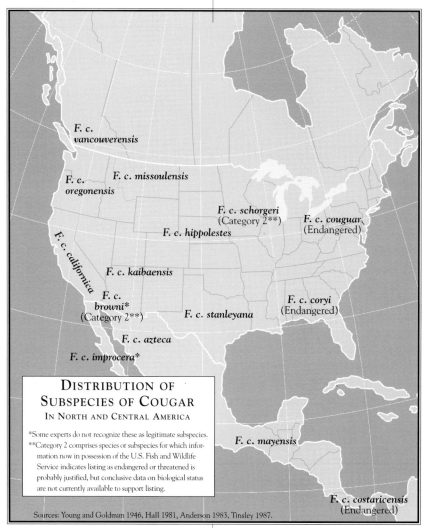

DISTRIBUTION OF SUBSPECIES OF COUGAR
IN NORTH AND CENTRAL AMERICA

*Some experts do not recognize these as legitimate subspecies.
**Category 2 comprises species or subspecies for which information now in possession of the U.S. Fish and Wildlife Service indicates listing as endangered or threatened is probably justified, but conclusive data on biological status are not currently available to support listing.

Sources: Young and Goldman 1946, Hall 1981, Anderson 1983, Tinsley 1987.

F. c. vancouverensis
F. c. oregonensis
F. c. missoulensis
F. c. schorgeri (Category 2**)
F. c. couguar (Endangered)
F. c. hippolestes
F. c. californica
F. c. kaibaensis
*F. c. browni** (Category 2**)
F. c. stanleyana
F. c. coryi (Endangered)
F. c. azteca
*F. c. improcera**
F. c. mayensis
F. c. costaricensis (Endangered)

CHAPTER 1. THE CONSUMMATE CAT (NOTES)

1. Seidensticker, J.C. 1991a. Pumas. Pages 130–138 *in* J. Seidensticker and S. Lumpkin, eds. *Great cats: Majestic creatures of the wild.* Rodale Press. Emmaus, Pennsylvania.

2. Sunquist, F.C. 1991. The living cats. Pages 28–53 *in* J. Seidensticker and S. Lumpkin, eds. *Great cats: Majestic creatures of the wild.* Rodale Press, Emmaus, Pennsylvania.

3. Morse, S.C. 1991. Forest Ecologist and Wildlife Habitat Consultant. Morse and Morse Forestry. Jericho, Vermont. (Personal communication)

4. Barnes, C.T. 1960. *The cougar or mountain lion.* Ralton Co., Salt Lake City.

5. Lynch, W. 1989. The elusive cougar. *Canadian Geographic* August/September: 24–31.

6. Young, S.P., and E.A. Goldman. 1946. *The puma: Mysterious American cat.* American Wildlife Institute, Washington, D.C.

7. Tinsley, J.B. 1987. *The puma: Legendary lion of the Americas.* Texas Western Press, The University of Texas at El Paso.

8. McMullen, J.P. 1984. *Cry of the panther: Quest of a species.* Pineapple Press, Englewood, Florida.

9. Guggisberg, C.A.W. 1975. *Wild cats of the world.* Taplinger Publishing Co., New York.

10. Hornocker, M.G. 1969b. Stalking the mountain lion—to save him. *National Geographic* November: 638–655.

11. Kitchener, A. 1991. *The natural history of the wild cats.* Cornell University Press. Ithaca, New York.

12. Neff, N.A. 1991. The cats and how they came to be. Pages 14–23 *in* J. Seidensticker and S. Lumpkin, eds. *Great cats: Majestic creatures of the wild.* Rodale Press. Emmaus, Pennsylvania,

13. Van Valkenburgh, B. 1991. Cats in communities: Past and present. Page 16 *in* J. Seidensticker and S. Lumpkin, eds. *Great cats: Majestic creatures of the wild.* Rodale Press. Emmaus, Pennsylvania.

14. Hornocker, M.G. C. Jonkel, and L.D. Mech. 1979. Family felidae. Mountain lion (*Felis concolor*). *Wild Animals of North America.* National Geographic, Washington, D.C.

15. O'Brien, S.J. 1991. Molecular evolution of cats. Page 18 *in* J. Seidensticker and S. Lumpkin, eds. *Great cats: Majestic creatures of the wild.* Rodale Press. Emmaus, Pennsylvania.

16. Seidensticker, J.C. 1991b. Introduction to "The living cats" by F.C. Sunquist. Page 28 *in* J. Seidensticker and S. Lumpkin, eds. *Great cats: Majestic creatures of the wild.* Rodale Press. Emmaus, Pennsylvania.

17. Shaw, H. 1989. *Soul among lions.* Johnson Books. Boulder, Colorado.

18. Anderson, A.E. 1983. *A critical review of literature on puma (Felis concolor).* Colorado Division of Wildlife. Special Report Number 54.

19. U.S. Fish and Wildlife Service. 1991. *Endangered and threatened wildlife and plants, 50 CFR 17.11 & 17.12, July 15, 1991.* U.S. Government Printing Office: 1991-296-520:50024. Washington D.C.

20. Duke, R., R. Klinger, R. Hopkins, and M. Kutilek. 1987. *Yuma puma (Felis concolor browni).* Feasibility Report Population Status Survey. 22 September 1987. Harvey and Stanley Associates, Inc. Alviso, California. Completed for the Bureau of Reclamation.

21. Currier, M.J.P. 1983. *Felis concolor.* Mammalian Species No. 200, pp. 1–7. American Society of Mammalogists.

22. Lindzey, F. 1987. Mountain lion. Pages 656–668 *in* M. Novak, J.A. Baker, M.E. Obbard, and M. Malloch, eds. *Wild furbearer management and conservation in North America.* Ministry of Natural Resources, Ontario, Canada.

23. Quigley, H. 1990. The complete cougar. *Wildlife Conservation* March/April: 67.

24. Collette, M. 1991. Founder and President, Wildlife Waystation, Angeles National Forest, California. (Personal communication)

25. Hopkins, R.A. 1991. Wildlife Biologist, H.T. Harvey and Associates, Alviso, California. (Personal communication)

THE CYCLE OF LIFE

BIRTH

Pregnant females do not prepare elaborate dens. It seems only to matter that it provides a refuge from predators (coyotes, golden eagles, other cougars) and shields the litter from heavy rain and hot sun. Dens rarely contain any bedding for the young, though a mother's soft belly hair was found in one.[2] (This also contradicts the popular misconception, perpetuated largely by some nature movies, that cougars always choose caves as dens.)[6]

Newborn mountain lions enter the world as buff brown balls of fur weighing slightly more than a pound.[1] Biologists call them kittens or cubs—either is correct. Their eyes and ear canals are closed, their coats are covered with blackish brown spots, and their tails are dark-ringed.[2] This color pattern provides excellent protective camouflage.

Kittens begin nursing within minutes after birth and gain weight rapidly, with males tending to outpace females.[1] Nursing mothers have eight teats but apparently only six produce milk.[3] Kittens start to compete for nipples the first day and generally suckle the same nipple whenever nursing.[4] At two weeks of age the kittens' eyes and ears are open and they are able to walk. Within 10 to 20 days the kittens may weigh over two pounds. They begin to move awkwardly about, exploring the rock overhang, brushy thicket, or pile of boulders that serves as their den.[5]

While suckling her young the mother must occasionally leave the den to hunt. This is the time of her most restricted movement, because she does not want to venture too far from her vulnerable kittens. Still, she must hunt to sustain herself and replenish her milk. While hunting, the female cougar remains within a fixed area called a *home range*. Varying in size from 25 to 400 square miles,[7,8] home ranges are restricted areas of use in which cougars confine their movements while hunting, searching out a mate, or raising young. Biologists refer to the cougars that occupy home ranges as *residents*. Possession of a home range is critically important to a female cougar because it increases her litter's chances for survival by guaranteeing an established hunting area for the mother.

By the time kittens are weaned at 2 to 3 months, the mother has moved the litter to one or more additional den sites throughout her home range. This provides greater protection for the young and may be one reason she does not construct elaborate dens. In his book *Soul Among Lions*, Arizona cougar specialist Harley Shaw explains that there are other advantages to such behavior: "…kittens learn early to move around their range and not imprint upon a single home site. Home is the entire area of use. Within it, lions are free to move, hunt, and rest as their mood and physiology directs. They are not handicapped by the human compulsion to return to a single safe base at night. Home is a large tract of land that they undoubtedly come to know as you and I know the floorplan of our house. They learn to be lions in this home area."[6]

The physical metamorphosis of young, growing cougars is dramatic, especially their teeth and coat. Teeth are critical to a cougar's survival, so the teeth in young cougars develop quickly. Their large canines (or fangs) allow them to capture and kill prey, while their specially adapted molars (called carnassials) are used to cut through tissue while feeding. Canines first appear at age 20 to 30 days, followed by the molars at 30 to 50 days. Permanent teeth start replacing primary (baby) teeth at about 5 1/2 months. The permanent canines first appear at month eight, and for a short time both permanent and primary canines are present.[3]

As an adult cougar's tawny coat provides camouflage

while stalking prey, a kitten's spots provide camouflage from predators. Kittens begin to lose these spots at 12 to 14 weeks, they fade rapidly but are still obvious at 8 months, less so at one year. By 15 months the markings are visible only on the hindquarters and only under certain light conditions. In some cougars, the stripes on the upper foreleg are still visible at 3 years of age.[3,9]

The mountain lion's coat is not the only feature that changes color with age. Their eyes, light blue at birth, begin to change at four months and are the golden brown of adults by 16 to 17 months.[3,9]

DETAIL OF COUGAR TEETH FOR AGING

Frontal view of upper incisors and canines of female and male cougars displaying relative wear by adult age classes.

gum line

FEMALE

MALE

10+ years
7-9 years
5-6 years
3-4 years
2 years

Source: Ashman et al. 1983; Lindzey 1987; Shaw 1987.

GROWING UP AND LEAVING HOME

Female cougars probably begin leading their kittens to kills as early as 7 to 8 weeks. The mother also carries meat to her young from kills until weaning age (2 to 3 months), at which point the cubs weigh in at between 7 and 9 pounds. As the kittens grow older, the mother will leave them at kills, frequently for days at a time, while she goes in search of the next prey.[6] As the kittens grow and become stronger, the mother will range farther in search of prey.

Biologists have frequently noted how intensely a female with kittens uses her home range. This is most concentrated subsequent to birth, then expands as the kittens are able to accompany her to kills. It's easy to imagine an insistent mother as she drags, pushes, and urges her kittens along over the many miles between kills. She expends an enormous amount of energy feeding her growing litter. As a result, the density of prey in the mother's home range affects how well she can provide for her young, which in turn influences their likelihood of survival.

Arrival at a kill is a time of both feeding and play for kittens. Vegetation is frequently disturbed for 50 feet surrounding the carcass. Grass is flattened, limbs are broken off trees and trunks are covered with the kittens' claw marks. The carcass is more fully consumed than it would be by an adult lion alone, and pieces of hair and bone are scattered about.[6] This rambunctious play by the young at a kill is another part of their training as predators. They will stalk, attack, and wrestle with their siblings or mother, as if they were the next meal rather than their own flesh and blood. Ultimately, though, play gives way to the real thing.

As they grow stronger and more skilled at stalking, kittens will separate from their mother for days at a time and hunt on their own. This growing independence is a precursor to young lions leaving their mother and going in search of their own home range. Biologists are not certain whether a mother and her young gradually grow apart, with the kittens finally leaving of their own accord, or whether she abandons them as do female black bears with their young. Sonny Bass has found the latter to be the case in Florida. "My experience with Florida panthers in the Everglades (based on daily tracking) indicates that the mother leaves the young."[10] Seidensticker tells of one Idaho cougar that abandoned her kittens at a kill.[11] Paul Beier, who studied mountain lions in southern California, believes the mother discourages her kittens from remaining with her. "Some sort of agonistic behavior on the part of the mother is necessary to discourage the young from staying. Simply abandoning the young is not possible because they know where to find her."[12] The presence of mature resident males attracted to the female, who by now is in heat, may also discourage the young from remaining. However they separate, the kittens are finally on their own and the mother will come into heat and breed again.[6]

Kittens can survive on their own as early as 6 months, such as when the mother is killed or dies of natural causes,[13] but this appears to be rare. Typically, the young cougars will remain with their mother for 12 to 18 months. This allows them to hone their hunting skills and gives them time to develop their killing bite.[14] This bite is usually delivered to the back of the neck of large prey, severing the spinal cord and causing almost immediate death. To be executed efficiently, the bite requires practice and development of the cougar's powerful jaw muscles. Evidence seems to indicate that the behavioral patterns of killing prey may be innate, but that selection of appropriate prey and stalking may require practice to acquire the necessary skill.[1, 2, 6] This may explain why young cougars are sometimes found with a face full of porcupine quills, or are the culprits in attacks on domestic livestock.

The departure of young cats from their mother's home range is called *dispersal*, and it is a time when the young cougars are especially vulnerable; they expose themselves to the dangers of taking prey without the alternative of food provided by their mother. These young cats, called *transients*, wander far from the familiar home range of their mother and their hunting skills are not as efficient as those of older resident cats. The dispersal of young transient cougars out of their birth areas is crucial, however, as it reduces inbreeding and provides new blood to outlying populations.[9]

MATING

Both male and female cougars are sexually mature at 24 months, but females have been known to breed as early as 20 months;[9] a Florida panther was recently reported as having given birth before she was 2 years old.[15] The age of the first breeding may be delayed until the female has established a home range.[16]

When it comes time to mate, the first challenge facing a male and female cougar is finding one another. Solitary and territorial by nature, cougars are frequently scattered over hundreds of miles of rugged terrain. It further complicates the matter that females are receptive to males for only a few days out of each month;[17] however, it appears to be the lions' territorial habits and keen senses that ultimately allow them to come together.

Polygamy seems to be the rule for both male and female mountain lions. Males occupy larger home ranges than females, and a resident male with a large home range typically overlaps or encompasses the home ranges of several resident females. Nevertheless, in stable cougar populations with established home ranges, females rarely mate with more than one resident male during a breeding cycle.[9]

Resident male cougars use *scrapes* as visual and olfactory signals to other cougars and to mark their home range area. A scrape (or scratch) is a collection of pine needles, leaves, or dirt scraped into a pile with either the forepaws or hindpaws. Occasionally they urinate or defecate on the pile. Scrapes are made throughout the home range and are frequently located along travelways under a tree[18,19] or along ridges. Females rarely scrape, more commonly burying their feces under mounds of dirt and debris; these mounds are usually found near large kills.[19]

Mountain lion authority Fred Lindzey believes scrapes help mountain lions both avoid and locate each other. "Scrapes are definitely a means of communication. They broadcast the resident male's presence to other males (residents and transients) and to females. Females may use scrapes made by the resident male to both avoid him when she has dependent kittens and to find him when she is in estrus." [20]

Adult males probably spend most of their time searching for receptive females.[21] When mating does occur, it usually takes place in the female's home range, with the male seeking out the female.[6] The female's estrous cycle lasts approximately 23 days and she is usually in heat for about 8 days. The pair may stay together for up to 3 days, sometimes even sharing a kill.[19]

Cougars compensate for long periods of solitude with some of the most vigorous breeding behavior known to exist among mammals. Copulation can occur at a rate of 50 to 70 times in 24 hours for a 7- to 8-day period.[22] Each copulation lasts less than a minute.[2] Such enthusiastic copulation is thought to stimulate ovulation, (the release of eggs from the ovaries to make them available for fertilization). In his book *The Natural History of the Wild Cats*, Andrew Kitchener explains the advantage of such behavior: "Most cats are thought to be induced ovulators, so that even though the female may come into estrus, no ovulation occurs unless the vagina and cervix of the female are stimulated repeatedly during mating. As a consequence of estrus lasting several days and ovulation being induced, the chances of a successful fertilization can be maximized."[23] Some biologists speculate that high copulation rates also evolved as a way for females to evaluate male vigor[1] and to ensure that their offspring receive the best genetic endowment.[24]

Cougars appear to be as vocal as they are enthusiastic during mating. The "caterwaul," characteristic in domestic cats, seems to be even louder in mating cougars. Such behavior has been documented both in captive and wild cougars.[9] Paul Beier has heard these sounds coming from mating cougars in his California study area;[12] biologist Susan de Treville, who studied mountain lions in California, was camping on the Malaspina Peninsula in British

Columbia when she heard two cougars mating nearby. "Both were screaming loudly. They got to within a foot of my tent, then they gradually moved off. In the morning I found the ground torn up and all the grass flattened."[25]

After 88 to 96 days, the mother retires to the seclusion of the den and gives birth to a litter of 1 to 6 kittens (or cubs). The average litter size is 2 to 3 kittens, but a young female may produce only 1 kitten in her first litter.[26] This seems to reduce the stress on first-time mothers, allowing them to develop their skills in rearing young. Since cougars tend to bear young every other year, a female that lives for 8 or 10 years has the potential to produce 5 litters. One captive cougar produced 7 litters in 16 years.[27] How many of the kittens survive to adulthood is still a mystery. It is also unknown if the number of offspring produced by a female cougar fluctuates in relation to the abundance of prey, as in other predators such as coyotes and barn owls. Few newly born litters have been studied closely in the wild, and definitive information is lacking; however, current research underway in Yellowstone National Park and in the San Andres Mountains of New Mexico may provide some answers about the early lives of pumas.

If a female loses her kittens to predators or other circumstances, she may begin her estrous cycle and breed again soon after the loss.[28] Sometimes, predators include male cougars; studies in Idaho, Utah, and California have documented that males do indeed kill and even eat kittens on occasion. Whether this is an evolved behavior similar to African lions is unknown, but it may partly explain why females with kittens are unreceptive to males and intolerant of their presence until the young are independent and can hunt for themselves. Females also seem to possess the ability to suppress their estrous cycle during the period they are raising young. Some experts speculate that this ability is hormonal in nature and is possibly related to lactation; others suggest that estrous cycles continue normally and the female simply works harder at avoiding males by being careful where she urinates and by burying her feces. Whether this behavior is hormonal, behavioral, or both is unknown.

Unlike most wild animals, cougars can and do give birth throughout the year, although peaks have been documented in different parts of their range. One population in Idaho peaked in the spring,[16] while cougars in parts of Utah[19] and Wyoming[29] had fall birth peaks. Nevada biologists documented birth peaks during June and July and noted 70 percent of all births occurred between April and September.[9] Mountain lions in and around Yellowstone National Park give birth primarily in midsummer.[30] Researcher Allen Anderson looked at the birth dates of 6 wild

and 35 captive cougars and discovered that over half (55 percent) of the births occured during April, June, July, and August.[1]

Biologists long speculated that in temperate climates, births occurring during the warmer months placed less stress on both the mother and kittens; however, as Harley Shaw points out, "Birth in warm months forces the mother to be feeding *large* young during mid to late winter. This does not reduce stress on her over the long haul."[31] It has also been suggested that in the warmer climates of Arizona, Florida, and California, births may be more evenly distributed throughout the year. Existing information from these states is inconclusive. Two more aspects of the American lion that have left experts scratching their heads.

DEATH

While all cougars enter the world in the same fashion, they leave it in a variety of ways. Existing information indicates that the three primary causes of cougar deaths are humans, natural causes, and accidents.

More mountain lions die at the hands of humans than any other known cause of death. This is as true today as it was in the past. A *minimum* of 65,665 cougars were shot, poisoned, trapped, and snared by bounty hunters, federal hunters, and sport hunters from 1907 to 1978 in the 12 western states, British Columbia, and Alberta.[32] This carnage seemed to peak between 1930 and 1955, with the highest numbers of pumas killed in California, British Columbia, and Arizona.[1] This sobering tally does not include the thousands of cougars slaughtered prior to the 1900s nor the untold numbers that have gone unreported since.

Today, cougar hunting is legal in Arizona, Colorado, Idaho, Montana, Nevada, New Mexico, Oregon, Texas, Utah, Washington, Wyoming, and the Canadian provinces of British Columbia and Alberta. During the 1989–1990 sport harvest season more than 2,176 cats were killed.[33] Most of these states allow hunters to kill only one lion per season, with the notable exception of Texas, which has the most liberal hunting regulations and places no limit on the number of cats a hunter can take. The cougar enjoys full protection in 24 states and provinces, but has no legal classification and no protection, except in agreement with the federal government, in 22 other states and provinces.[3,32] (The legal status of the cougar in the United States and Canada will be discussed more fully in Chapter 6.)

Predator control programs present yet another obstacle to the cougar's survival. The U.S. Department of Agriculture's Animal Damage Control (ADC) program was responsible for killing 207 cougars in 11 western states during the 1988 fiscal year because of attacks on domestic livestock.[34] In addition to ADC's efforts, many states carry on their own predator control programs. For instance, in 1988, ADC killed 38 cougars in California, while the state Department of Fish and Game authorized other hunters to take an additional 28 cougars on depredation permits, for a total of 64 cats. This situation is further complicated by the fact that cougars are occasionally caught in traps set for other animals, and because there is no easy way to release them many are killed. The cats can sometimes pull themselves free of the traps, often at the cost of severed toes or broken bones. Cats that escape with minor injuries may still be capable of taking large prey and surviving, while those with debilitating injuries likely die of starvation.[9]

Collisions with motor vehicles are the primary cause of death in Florida panthers. From 1979 to 1991, almost 50 percent of documented mortality of the Florida cats was due to collisions with autos.[35] In California, 22 mountain lions fell victim to collisions between 1971 and 1976,[7] while researcher Paul Beier lost five lions he was studying to cars.[12] Three young cougars were even killed by a train, all in the same incident, in Colorado.[1]

A number of the cats have drowned in irrigation canals,[36] or by falling into wells.[37] Cougars are capable swimmers, but the smooth concrete banks make escape dif-

ficult and the exhausted cats will eventually drown. Unfortunately, such incidents will increase as more cougar habitat is encroached upon by humans.

Even in the absence of humans, cougars practice a high-risk lifestyle; they are continuously exposed to risk of injury or death because they prey on animals larger than they are. In Idaho, both male and female pumas kill adult male elk, an animal seven times the size of a female puma.[38] While deer, more manageable in size, are the cougar's prey of choice, some do not submit without a struggle. During attacks on deer or elk cougars have been thrown against trees so hard that their backs have been broken or they sustained massive internal injuries. They have been trampled by the hooves of deer and elk they were attacking, and even impaled on branches or antlers.[39] A debilitating injury like a broken bone can lead to starvation.

Other types of accidents include falls from cliffs, being struck by lightning, being hit by rock slides, being poisoned by venomous snakes, and choking.[3] Susan de Treville tells of a mountain lion that died from a violent encounter with a manzanita bush! "We were monitoring an old lion (9–10 years) named Snaggletooth, because he had a broken upper canine. One day we found him lying in an open field— dead. We had no idea what killed him. Later, an examination revealed a 5-inch piece of manzanita in the cat's throat. Apparently, during the final rush at what we think was a deer, the cat ran into a manzanita bush at high speed, driving a stob down its throat and severing the carotid artery. Failing eyesight may have been part of the reason. Snaggletooth bled to death internally."[25]

There are three times during their lives when cougars are most at risk: immediately after birth, immediately after becoming independent transients, and during old age.[3] Kittens left alone at a den or kill are vulnerable to other predators, including, as has been noted, adult male cougars; it is unknown how many kittens survive to maturity, but experts suspect that kitten deaths could equal or exceed the

number of cougars killed by sport hunting. Transient cougars spend most of their time in unfamiliar territory and have not honed their hunting skills, so do not hunt as efficiently as resident cougars. Old cougars experience extreme tooth wear and loss of weight, making them less efficient hunters, resulting in starvation. Old age is probably the most significant cause of death in unhunted mountain lion populations; a recent study in southern Utah showed that the annual mortality rate in an unhunted cougar population was a fairly high 26 percent.[26] In Montana's hunted cougar populations, over 50 percent of the resident adults in one area were killed, according to research conducted there.[40]

Adult cougars do kill and even eat one another on occasion.[1] Fighting has been documented in Arizona, California, Nevada, Texas, Wyoming, and Utah. In one study in the San Andres Mountains of southern New Mexico, fighting was found to be the primary cause of death.[41] While in Florida, fighting has led to the death of six endangered panthers over the past 11 years. Of these, two were transient males dispersing from their mother's home range through home ranges of resident males courting females in heat; two were adult females killed by a young adult male; and the last two were the result of fighting between adult males.[35] Experts speculate that most conflicts are over females and home ranges, but it is still unknown precisely how much fighting contributes to overall mortality in a cougar population.

Cougars appear to suffer from relatively few internal and external parasites. Those they do contend with include an assortment of fleas, ticks, mites, and tapeworms. The puma's solitary lifestyle and its habit of spending little time in dens probably minimizes infestation.[2,3]

Deaths attributable to more serious diseases appear to be uncommon. Only two cases of rabies have been documented in wild mountain lions, one in California in 1909,[42] and a more recent case in Florida.[35] Naturally occurring antibodies to feline distemper were found in 85 percent of the Florida panthers tested.[43] Another mountain lion in California was recently diagnosed with feline leukemia and was killed. California Department of Fish and Game veterinarian Thierry Work thinks the cat may have been infected by eating domestic cats. The feline leukemia virus is frequently fatal and no vaccine for wild cougars exists; this disease especially threatens small, isolated populations of cougars that front on urban areas, such as in southern Florida and southern California. Allen Anderson cautions that the widely held opinion that wild pumas are largely free of parasites and diseases may be due to the lack of specific research rather than reality.[1] Cougar diseases are just one of many aspects of the cat that need further study.

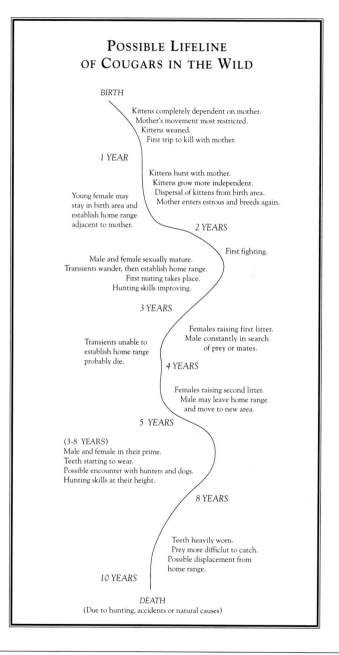

POSSIBLE LIFELINE OF COUGARS IN THE WILD

BIRTH
Kittens completely dependent on mother.
Mother's movement most restricted.
Kittens weaned.
First trip to kill with mother.

1 YEAR
Young female may stay in birth area and establish home range adjacent to mother.

Kittens hunt with mother.
Kittens grow more independent.
Dispersal of kittens from birth area.
Mother enters estrous and breeds again.

2 YEARS
First fighting.

Male and female sexually mature.
Transients wander, then establish home range.
First mating takes place.
Hunting skills improving.

3 YEARS

Females raising first litter.
Male constantly in search of prey or mates.

Transients unable to establish home range probably die.

4 YEARS

Females raising second litter.
Male may leave home range and move to new area.

5 YEARS

(3-8 YEARS)
Male and female in their prime.
Teeth starting to wear.
Possible encounter with hunters and dogs.
Hunting skills at their height.

8 YEARS

Teeth heavily worn.
Prey more difficult to catch.
Possible displacement from home range.

10 YEARS

DEATH
(Due to hunting, accidents or natural causes)

CHAPTER 2. THE CYCLE OF LIFE (NOTES)

1. Anderson, A.E. 1983. *A critical review of literature on puma (Felis concolor)*. Colorado Division of Wildlife. Special Report Number 54.

2. Dixon, K.R. 1982. Mountain lion. Pages 711–727 in J.A. Chapman and G.A. Feldhamer, eds. *Wild mammals of North America*. John Hopkins University Press. Baltimore.

3. Currier, M.J.P. 1983. *Felis concolor*. Mammalian Species No. 200, pp. 1–7. American Society of Mammalogists.

4. Eaton, R.L. and K.A. Velander. 1977. Reproduction in the puma: Biology, behavior and ontogeny. Pages 45–70 in R.L. Eaton, ed. *The world's cats, Vol. 3(3): Contributions to breeding biology, behavior and husbandry*. Carnivore Research Institute, University of Washington, Seattle.

5. Young, S.P., and E.A. Goldman. 1946. *The puma: Mysterious American cat*. American Wildlife Institute, Washington, D.C.

6. Shaw, H. 1989. *Soul among lions*. Johnson Books. Boulder, Colorado.

7. Sitton, L.W. and S. Wallen. 1976. *California mountain lion study*. California Department of Fish and Game. Sacramento.

8. Hemker, T.P., F.G. Lindzey, and B.B. Ackerman. 1984. Population characteristics and movement patterns of cougars in southern Utah. *Journal of Wildlife Management*, 48(4):1275–1284.

9. Lindzey, F. 1987. Mountain lion. Pages 656–668 in M. Novak, J.A. Baker, M.E. Obbard, and B. Malloch, eds. *Wild furbearer management and conservation in North America*. Ministry of Natural Resources, Ontario, Canada.

10. Bass, O.L. 1991. Wildlife Biologist, Everglades National Park Research Center, Homestead, Florida. (Personal communication)

11. Turbak, G. and A. Carey. 1986. *America's great cats*. Northland Publishing, Flagstaff, Arizona.

12. Beier, P. 1992b. Project Leader, Orange County Cooperative Mountain Lion Study, Department of Forestry and Resource Management, University of California, Berkeley. (Personal communication)

13. Hornocker, M.G. and G.M. Koehler. 1985. Reintroducing orphaned mountain lion kittens into the wild. Pages 167–169 in J. Roberson and F. Lindzey, eds. *Proceedings of the second mountain lion workshop*, Salt Lake City.

14. Bogue, G. and M. Ferrari. 1974. The predatory "training" of captive reared pumas. Pages 36–45 in R.L. Eaton, ed. *The world's cats, Vol. 3(1): Contributions to status, management and conservation*. Carnivore Research Institute, University of Washington, Seattle. (Cited from Dixon 1982.)

15. Maehr, D.S., J.C. Roof, E.D. Land, and J.W. McCown. 1989. First reproduction of a panther (*Felis concolor coryi*) in southwestern Florida. *Mammalia*, 53:129–131.

16. Seidensticker, J.C., IV, M.G. Hornocker, W.V. Wiles, and J.P. Messick. 1973. Mountain lion social organization in the Idaho Primative Area. *Wildlife Monographs*, 35.

17. Rabb, G.G. 1959. Reproductive and vocal behavior in captive pumas. *Journal of Mammalogy*. 49:616–617. (Cited from Dixon 1982.)

18. Shaw, H. 1987. *Mountain lion field guide*. 3rd Edition. Special Report Number 9. Arizona Game and Fish Department.

19. Hemker, T.P. 1982. Population characteristics and movement patterns of cougars in southern Utah. M.S. thesis, Utah State University, Logan.

20. Lindzey, F.G. 1991. Wildlife Biologist, U.S. Fish and Wildlife Service, Wyoming Cooperative Fish and Wildlife Research Unit, University of Wyoming, Laramie, Wyoming. (Personal communication)

21. Hopkins, R.A. 1991. Wildlife Biologist, H.T. Harvey and Associates, Alviso, California. (Personal communication)

22. Eaton, R.L. 1976. Why some felids copulate so much. *World's cats*. 3:73–94. (Cited from Anderson 1983.)

23. Kitchener, A. 1991. *The natural history of the wild cats*. Cornell University Press. Ithaca, New York.

24. Lynch, W. 1989. The elusive cougar. *Canadian Geographic* August/September: 24–31.

25. de Treville, S. 1991. Wildlife Biologist. de Treville Environmental Engineering. San Diego, California. (Personal communication)

26. Lindzey, F.G., B.B. Ackerman, D. Barnhurst, T. Becker, T.P. Hemker, S.P. Laing, C. Mecham, and W.D. Van Sickle. 1989. *Boulder-Escalante cougar project final report*. Utah Division of Wildlife Resources, Salt Lake City, Utah.

27. Conklin, W.A. 1884. *The mammals of the Adirondack Region, northeastern New York*. L.S. Foster Press, New York. (Cited from Dixon 1982.)

28. Hornocker, M.G.. 1970. An analysis of mountain lion predation upon mule deer and elk in the Idaho Primative Area. *Wildlife Monographs*. 21:1–39.

29. Logan, K.A. 1983. Mountain lion population and habitat characteristics in the Big Horn Mountains of Wyoming. M.S. thesis, University of Wyoming, Laramie.

30. Murphy, K. 1991. Wildlife Biologist. Wildlife Research Institute, Inc., Moscow, Idaho. (Personal communication)

31. Shaw, H. 1991. Wildlife Biologist, General Wildlife Services, Chino Valley, Arizona. (Personal communication)

32. Nowak, R.M. 1976. *The cougar in the United States and Canada.* New York Zoological Society and U.S. Fish and Wildlife Service Office of Endangered Species, Washington, D.C.

33. Tully, R.J. 1991. *Summary of 1991 questionnaire on mountain lion hunting regulations.* Mountain Lion-Human Interaction Symposium and Workshop, April 24–26, Denver. Colorado Division of Wildlife.

34. U.S. Department of Agriculture. 1990. Animal and Plant Health Inspection Service. *Animal damage control program, draft environmental impact statement-1990.*

35. Maehr, D.S., E.D. Land, and M.E. Roelke. 1991b. Mortality patterns of panthers in southwest Florida. *Proceedings of the annual conference of southeast fish and wildlife agencies.* 45:In press.

36. Macgregor, W.G. 1976. The status of the puma in California. Pages 28–35 *in* R.L. Eaton, ed. *The world's cats, Vol. 3(1): Contributions to status, management and conservation.* Carnivore Research Institute, University of Washington, Seattle. (Cited from Dixon 1982.)

37. Sitton, L.W. and R.A. Weaver. 1977. *California mountain lion investigations with recommendations for management.* California Department of Fish and Game, Sacramento.

38. Seidensticker, J.C. 1991a. Pumas. Pages 130–138 *in* J. Seidensticker and S. Lumpkin, eds. *Great cats: Majestic creatures of the wild.* Rodale Press. Emmaus, Pennsylvania.

39. Lopez, B. 1981. The elusive mountain lion. GEO June: 98–116.

40. Murphy, K. 1983. *Characteristics of a hunted population of mountain lions in western Montana. (Relationships between a mountain lion population and hunting pressure in western Montana.)* Report to the Montana Department of Fish, Wildlife and Parks.

41. Logan, K.A. 1991. Wildlife Research Institute, Inc., Moscow, Idaho. (Personal communication)

42. Storer, T.I. 1923. Rabies in a mountain lion. *California Fish and Game.* April 9(2):45–48.

43. Roelke, M.E. 1987. *Florida panther biomedical investigation. Annual performance report.* Endangered Species Project E-1-11. Florida Game and Fresh Water Fish Commission. (Cited from Belden 1989.)

COUGARS AT HOME

WHERE COUGARS LIVE

Biologists marvel at the cougar's remarkable adaptability. The best example of this is the cat's enormous geographic range. Cougars seem equally at home in Alberta's alpine forests, Arizona's Sonoran Desert, or Mexico's tropical jungles. While the lions don't seem particular about where they live, studies show that the cats do prefer certain types of terrain and vegetation. Habitat, a space and an environment suited to a particular species, and geographic range, a broader term indicating the map area in which a species occurs, are important concepts in understanding cougar life.[1] One expects to find cougars only in suitable habitats within a geographic range, and suitable cougar habitat contains two elements: cover and large prey.

Mountain lions are stalking predators that must get close to their prey before ambushing from a short distance. They will take advantage of terrain (steep canyons, rock outcroppings, boulders) or vegetation (dense brush, thickets) to remain hidden while stalking. *Cover* refers to this combination of terrain and vegetation that allows the cat to stay out of sight while hunting and stalking; habitats that have good *stalking cover* attract mountain lions. Cover also helps protect the female cougar's vulnerable kit-

tens. (In the previous chapter I explained how a dense thicket or pile of boulders is used as a den. This is what we mean by *protective cover*.)

Even the best stalking cover is of no value, however, if there is nothing to stalk. Deer are the lion's primary prey—mule deer in western North America and white-tailed deer in eastern North America[2]—and deer must be present in sufficient numbers in the lion's habitat for the cat to survive.[3] While lions will take a variety of prey, killing one deer is more energy-efficient than killing several rabbits or squirrels, allowing the cat to procure a lot of fresh meat at once. This is particularly important to females with hungry kittens to feed. Since the presence of cougars in an area is largely dependent on the presence of deer, it is important to understand what makes up good deer habitat.

Like cougar habitat, suitable deer habitat must contain a combination of cover and food. But because deer are ungulates (hoofed, plant-eating mammals) they use both resources differently. Where the puma requires stalking cover, deer need *escape cover*, usually a dense tangle of vegetation into which predators cannot easily follow.[1] In the case of desert bighorn sheep (*Ovis canadensis*), on which cougars occasionally prey in New Mexico, Nevada, and California, escape cover may not be "cover" in the normal sense, but a sheer rock face. The steep incline and exposure discourages a cougar from following and allows the sheep to escape.

Other types of cover are required. Deer need cover for giving birth to fawns and for resting (*protective cover* and *resting cover*). They cope with seasonal temperature extremes by taking refuge in timber stands (*thermal cover*); tall trees with dense foliage reduce heat loss through radiation on cold, clear winter nights, provide shade on hot sunny days, and serve as shields from strong winds for deer and cougars alike.[4]

Being herbivores (plant-eaters), deer will gravitate to habitats that have adequate forage. Mule deer (*Odocoileus hemionus*), the most common species of deer in the western United States and Canada, require a mix of food types[5] and are known to eat 788 plant species.[6] In southern Utah, mule deer feed extensively on bitterbrush and Gambel oak, two plants that also provide excellent cover. Not surprisingly, areas dominated by these two plants are also frequented by mountain lions.[7]

Maurice Hornocker[8] and later John Seidensticker and his coworkers[9] studied cougars in the remote wilderness of the Idaho Primitive Area (now the Frank Church River of No Return Wilderness). There, they found that cougars preferred steep, rocky areas covered with dense stands of Douglas fir and ponderosa pine, with sagebrush and grasslands mixed among the bluffs and talus slopes. The big cats avoided crossing large open areas with insufficient cover, preferring to travel around the perimeters.

Researchers Kenny Logan and Larry Irwin[10] studied cougars in the Bighorn Mountains of northern Wyoming; their work provided the first quantified evaluation of cougar habitat use, and their findings were similar to those of Seidensticker and Hornocker in Idaho. The cats frequented canyonland habitats with steep, rugged slopes (greater than 45 degrees) containing mixed conifer and brushy mountain mahogany cover. Grasslands and sagebrush areas with gentle slopes (less than 20 degrees) were generally avoided.

The late Steven Laing was a member of a team of researchers who studied cougars in the Boulder-Escalante region of south-central Utah. This 10-year study, completed in 1989, is considered to be the most thorough examination of the cats yet completed. Laing, being responsible for examining cougar habitat use, found that cougars selected pinyon-juniper woodlands with lava boulders scattered in the understory cover (ground vegetation). The cats also frequented ponderosa pine/oakbrush, mixed aspen/spruce-fir, and spruce-fir habitats. These areas were typically at higher elevations with steeper slopes and denser understory cover. They avoided sagebrush bottomlands, agricultural and pasture lands, slickrock sandstone canyons, and open meadows. This combination of terrain and vegetation seems to enhance the cat's ability to survey and move through the landscape unseen.[7]

Harley Shaw observed a similar pattern in Arizona. Forested areas such as those found on the Mogollon Rim and Kaibab Plateau have little understory cover and hold relatively low mountain lion densities, while chaparral and pinyon-juniper vegetations, which have dense understory cover, have higher densities of mountain lions. Shaw suspects understory cover for stalking is the key to habitat suitability.[11]

Seidensticker and his colleagues[9] described suitable cougar habitat as a combination of vegetation, topography, prey numbers, and prey vulnerability. Prey vulnerability refers to the ease with which prey species may be captured and killed by cougars and depends on the availability of cover (both stalking cover and escape cover) and the behavior of the prey. The relationship between vegetation and prey vulnerability is particularly important: cougars cannot successfully take prey if there is too much or too little cover. The best vegetation for stalking cover is moderately dense—thick enough for the lion to remain hidden, sparse enough for the cat to see its prey.[12] Thus, the presence of moderately dense stalking cover in a habitat increases the vulnerability of the prey found there. This also explains why dense vegetation is attractive to deer as escape cover—it reduces their vulnerability to cougars.

Writer Barry Lopez calls the cougar "a dweller on the edge." Edges, or *ecotones*, are transitional borders between different habitat types—the places where forest meets clearing, where rocky ledge meets brush, and where willow thicket meets streamside banks.[2,13] Such areas provide good forage and cover for deer, which in turn attracts cougars. Florida panthers make frequent use of ecotones in Everglades National Park;[14] much of the panthers' habitat in that part of south Florida is slash pine woodland with dense understory cover of saw palmetto. This woodland forms the eastern boundary of a flat, grassy wetland (the Everglades) dotted with islands of hardwood trees called hammocks. Panthers do most of their hunting and make most of their kills along the edges of these hammocks and in these woodlands. Laing found a similar pattern in the Boulder-Escalante study: "Riparian zones [streamside habitats] and rock ledges were the two ecotones most associated with highly used areas…suggesting habitat selection based on prey densities, cover diversity, and possibly water availability."[7]

To a cougar, vegetation shape and density seems to be more important than vegetation type in determining habitat suitability. This partly explains the cat's ability to occupy such an extensive range and variety of habitats.[12]

So, the best deer and cougar habitats appear to be forested areas that contain good deer forage and cover as well as a diversity of terrain and sufficient stalking cover. Cougars seem consciously to select cover and terrain that allow them to find prey, observe it while stalking, and approach close enough to make a kill.[4] Seidensticker's study in Idaho[9] showed that, over a span of years, kill sites were clustered in certain areas, which suggested that these areas offered advantages in taking prey.

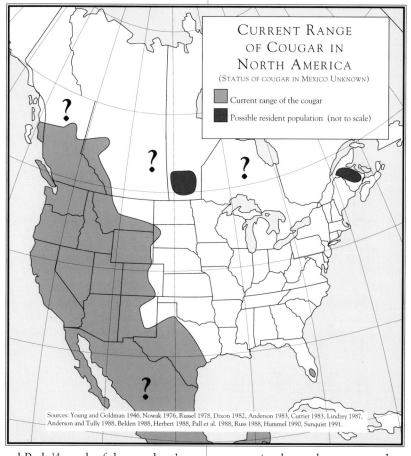

CURRENT RANGE
OF COUGAR IN
NORTH AMERICA
(STATUS OF COUGAR IN MEXICO UNKNOWN)

Current range of the cougar

Possible resident population (not to scale)

Sources: Young and Goldman 1946, Nowak 1976, Russel 1978, Dixon 1982, Anderson 1983, Currier 1983, Lindzey 1987, Anderson and Tully 1988, Belden 1988, Herbert 1988, Pall et al. 1988, Russ 1988, Hummel 1990, Sunquist 1991.

HOME RANGE

Within mountain lion habitat, adult cougars space themselves out and confine their movement to individual fixed areas known as *home ranges*. Home range should not be confused with geographic range, which is a broader term indicating the entire map area in which cougars occur.[1]

Cougar home ranges include hunting areas, water sources, resting areas, lookout positions, and denning sites where kittens or cubs can be safely reared. Cougars that occupy home ranges are called *residents*, and possession of a home range enhances a resident lion's chances of more consistently finding prey, locating mates, and successfully rearing young.[15]

Possession of a home range is fundamental to the cougar's survival as a solitary predator. By having a fixed area of land to hunt in, the cougar is better able to consistently locate prey. It roams its home range constantly, learning the terrain, where the best cover is, where the deer most likely can be found. This is why survival for a transient cougar is more precarious than that of a resident cougar. Transients are constantly moving through unfamiliar terrain and have not yet perfected their hunting skills.

Cougars are not territorial in the sense that they defend their home ranges to exclude all other cougars. Rather, the big cats have evolved a *land tenure* system[9] in

which home ranges are maintained by resident lions but not transient lions.[2] Male home ranges are typically larger than female home ranges, usually overlapping or encompassing several of the female ranges, but only occasionally overlapping those of other resident males; however, female home ranges commonly overlap.[12] Exceptions to this pattern do exist. Studies in the Diablo Mountains of California[16] and the San Andres Mountains of New Mexico[17] showed overlap between male home ranges, while those of females did not.

In areas where home ranges overlap, cougars seem to avoid each other. This *mutual avoidance*[8] is thought to be accomplished primarily through sight and smell.[2,12] Smell is employed through the use of scrapes. In the previous chapter it was explained how scrapes function as biological traffic signals within home ranges. By either making a scrape or sniffing the scrape of other individuals, cougars send and receive a variety of messages. Male residents can announce their presence, transient lions or females with dependent kittens can avoid male residents, and females can find males when they are ready to mate.[18] Two cougars with overlapping home ranges can both use the common area because scrapes allow them to use the area at different times.

After sniffing a scrape impregnated with the urine of

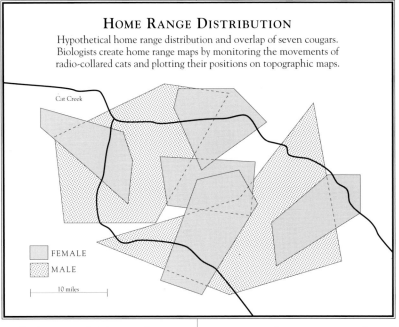

HOME RANGE DISTRIBUTION

Hypothetical home range distribution and overlap of seven cougars. Biologists create home range maps by monitoring the movements of radio-collared cats and plotting their positions on topographic maps.

Cat Creek

FEMALE
MALE

10 miles

another cougar, a lion will display a lip-curling grimace known as a *flehman*. This action is thought to allow them to use a special olfactory organ in the roof of their mouth to better evaluate, or get a better "look" at the scent. Biologists speculate that males may use the flehman to determine from a female's urine whether she is ready to mate.[9,19, 20] Both Seidensticker[9] and Lindzey[18] have observed this behavior in captive mountain lions.

Experts speculate that land tenure and mutual avoidance allow cougars to maintain home ranges in a number of beneficial ways. First, they seem to reduce conflict. A large, powerful carnivore like the cougar depends exclusively on its good health to capture prey. Frequent fighting could lead to serious injury and starvation. This is not to say fighting between cats never occurs; as has already been pointed out, in some cougar populations, such as in southern New Mexico, fighting is common and even a major source of mortality.[17] Secondly, maintaining a matrix of adjacent and overlapping home ranges seems to limit cougar population density,[8, 21, 22] which in turn increases the cats' chances of finding prey.

Finally, because home ranges are frequently hundreds of square miles in size, it would be impossible for a cougar to actively defend the entire area against all intruders.[15] As a result, a more flexible system of coexistence has evolved.

Researchers have learned much of what they know about home ranges through radio telemetry. This involves capturing a wild cougar and attaching a collar containing a small radio transmitter. By plotting the cat's locations on a topographic map, biologists can learn the size of the area a cougar uses throughout the year, what the density of cats in an area is, and the social structure of the population.[23] What they have learned is that home ranges vary widely in size, depending on local vegetation, prey density, and the time of year. Male home range size can vary from 25 to 500 square miles, while females usually occupy smaller areas of from 8 to over 400 square miles. Sitton and Wallen documented some of the smallest home ranges in the Big Sur region of coastal California, where the average home ranges were 25 to 35 square miles for males and 18 to 25 square miles for females.[24] A warmer climate and abundant

FLEHMAN RESPONSE

After sniffing a scape impregnated with urine of another cougar, a lion will display a lip-curling grimace known as a *flehman*. This apparently allows them to use a special olfactory organ in the roof of their mouth to get a better "look" at the scent.

forage probably make it unnecessary for the deer to migrate between winter and summer range and the herds thus concentrate in specific areas. Consequently, the cougar population concentrates around the denser prey population. The presence of good stalking cover is likely a factor as well.

Hemker and his colleagues found some of the largest home ranges during the Boulder-Escalante study in southern Utah, where males occupied areas of up to 513 square miles and females up to 426 square miles. [25]

As might be suspected, male and female cougars use their home ranges differently. Besides a place to hunt, males require an area where they can mate with as many females as possible without interference from surrounding males. This is why male home ranges overlap two, three, or more female home ranges and why male home ranges usually do not overlap. Female home ranges are usually smaller and are used to provide sufficient prey and denning sites for rearing kittens, even in years of low prey density. [15]

Life is tough for a female cougar—much tougher than for a male. Seidensticker explains why: "Adult females are subject to more stress and hazards than are males. The female must hunt and kill large, potentially dangerous prey more frequently than males and must do so at regular, predictable intervals if she is to succeed in rearing her kittens, thus increasing the likelihood of accidental death." [9] On occasion, males have even been known to abandon their home range and move to a new area; [26] older males can also be displaced from their home ranges by prime males. [17] Females show much more attachment to their home ranges and tend to remain in the same area for their entire lives.

The amount of stalking cover and prey numbers in cougar habitat obviously influence home range size. Home range size and the degree of overlap in turn influence the density of a cougar population in a given area. [27] Density estimates of 3 to 7 adult cougars per 100 square miles have been made in southern Alberta [28] and 5 to 8 adult cougars per 100 square miles in the Diablo Mountains of California. [16] Both habitats are characterized by good stalking cover and abundant prey. Lion densities in dryer desert climates seem to be lower. Linda Sweanor and

ESTIMATED HOME RANGES

Estimated home ranges (square miles) of 27 male and 40 female cougars from seven states from radio telemetry and mark-recapture studies.

State	Year	Season	Male			Female		
			Min	Max	Mean	Min	Max	Mean
Idaho [1]	1970-71	Summer-Fall	114	—	—	41	80	57
	1970-71	All year	176	—	—	67	145	104
	1970-72	Winter-Spring	16	85	49	12	94	41
	1964-68	Winter-Spring	25	—	—	—	—	—
	1964-68	Winter	—	—	—	5	20	13
Arizona [2]	1972-73	Winter	55	91	73	26	—	—
Nevada [3]	1972-73	All year	70	100	82	—	—	—
	1975-78	All year	131	276	186	55	—	—
	1978-79	Varies by cougar	179	301	86	21	45	30
New Mexico [4]	1975-77	All year	45	95	70	—	—	—
	1976-78	All year	—	—	—	22	75	47
California [5]	1976	Summer-Fall	50	—	—	20	40	27
	1979-80	All year	42	92	59	22	29	25
Utah [6]	1979-81	Nonwinter	—	—	222	—	—	134
		Winter	—	—	197	—	—	91
		Annual	—	—	320	—	—	165
Wyoming [7]	1981-83	All year	—	—	124	—	—	26

Sources: [1] Seidensticker et al. 1973, Hornocker 1969; [2] Shaw 1973; [3] Ashman 1975, 1978, 1979; [4] Bavin 1976, 1978; [5] Sitton 1977, Kutilek 1980; [6] Hemker 1984; [7] Logan 1983.

Kenney Logan estimate only 2 adult cougars per 100 square miles in their New Mexico study area, which lies in the Chihuahuan Desert.[29] Densities in southern Utah were even lower, at .5 to .8 adult cougars per 100 square miles, which was 30 percent lower than densities estimated elsewhere.[25] When stalking cover, prey, and water are scarce, cougars expend more energy searching for and stalking prey in larger home ranges. As a result, the cougar population is scattered more thinly across the region. (Fred Lindzey cautions that estimating densities of a solitary and highly mobile predator like the mountain lion is difficult, and that a variety of estimation methods are used by biologists, so one must be careful in making comparisons.[12])

As a result of the functions of land tenure and mutual avoidance, cougars appear to "saturate" an area at a given density. Research indicates that the density of cougars in a particular area is socially regulated through home range size and overlap and does not increase above a level socially tolerable for cougars. In other words, healthy cougar populations appear to be self-regulating. Harley Shaw explains: "In all studies of lions where relatively good documentation of lion numbers has been made, lion densities have peaked and stabilized at points between ten and twenty square miles per adult resident. Evidence indicates that, if left alone, adult resident lions will probably not populate beyond such densities."[22]

POPULATION DYNAMICS

Wildlife biologists have long puzzled over the cougar's solitary life style and how it benefits the animal as a predator. "I find it curious that an animal starting in a litter becomes antisocial in adulthood," writes Harley Shaw. "The earliest moments of a lion's life involve touching its siblings. Its growth involves play, interaction, and cooperation during early efforts in hunting. Yet the animal ultimately comes to avoid other adults except at breeding time."[22]

The cooperative hunting methods of wolves have been extensively studied and their success is well known, as is their gregarious life style. One cannot help but wonder if in comparison the cougar's solitary life style, especially hunting, puts the cat at a distinct disadvantage. Seidensticker and his fellow researchers don't think so: "The mountain lion, too, kills large potentially dangerous prey, but unlike the wolf, a pursuit predator, the lion is a stalking predator whose success depends solely on the element of surprise. In the broken land where lions find sufficient cover to stalk and launch successful attacks, the prey usually are scattered and time-consuming to find. Under such conditions, a solitary social structure is apparently the most effective life style."[9]

While hunting alone may have its advantages, cougars may not be as solitary as once thought. Rick Hopkins points out that adult males are not solitary by choice and probably spend most of their time searching for receptive females.[27] Susan de Treville once monitored four radio-collared males resident males to within 50 yards of each other in the Big Sur region of California.[30] Andrew Kitchener writes: "...far from having a chaotic, random system of home ranges driven by the need for [solitary] cats to avoid each other at all costs, most wild cats maintain a predictable system of land tenure, which promotes social stability and maximizes the reproductive success of both males and females...Far from being strangers, neighboring cats probably know each other very well from their own distinctive smells."[15]

Solitary or not, cougars that inhabit a common geographic area are referred to as a *population*,[1] and within a population not all cougars are created equal. This feline social hierarchy consists of three classes of animals: resident adult males and females, transient males and females, and dependent offspring of resident females. Resident adults maintain established home ranges and do most of the breeding in a population. Transients constantly move through the home ranges of residents in search of a vacant home range of their own;[12,23] while female transients tend to delay breeding until they find and occupy a home range, this may not be true of males.[14] Dependent offspring include kittens and juveniles that still rely on their mother to hunt for them.[23]

Determining whether a cougar is an adult, transient, or kitten is more complex than it sounds; finding a reliable way to determine age is something that has long eluded biologists. Age is usually estimated using a combination of tooth wear, body weight, coat spotting, and behavior. Kittens are newborn to 16 months old and are still with their mother in her home range; they may still have spots, which fade by the third or fourth month. Transients are 17 to 23 months old and have left their mother's home range but have not yet settled in a home range of their own; spotting may still be present on the insides of the front legs. Resident adults are mature cats, at least 24 months old, and occupy an established home range; spotting is absent or very faint, and females may show evidence of nursing.[26]

Harley Shaw uses a slightly different system of classify-

ing lions. Resident lions are adult males and females that use established home ranges and are reproductively active. Immature lions are defined as offspring of resident adults that are still traveling with, or close to, the mother. Transient lions are young, newly independent adults searching for a home range.[31]

Researchers Kenny Logan and Linda Sweanor prefer the terms emigrant and disperser to transient. These refer to lions that have emigrated or dispersed from their birth area but have not set up a home range. This dispersal out of a previously occupied area is called *emigration*, while movement into a new area is called *immigration*.[1] Emigrants become immigrants when they enter a new population.[17] (While it is good science for researchers to refine their techniques and terms, the lack of consistency also makes it difficult for scientists to compare information. It also frustrates writers attempting to explain mountain lions.)

Because no reliable method yet exists for accurately aging cougars, determining how many resident adults, transients, and kittens are present in a cougar population at any given time is equally difficult. This is further complicated

CLASSES OF COUGARS WITHIN A POPULATION

A typical cougar population consists of resident adult males and females, transient males and females, and dependent kittens of resident females. Transients are constantly moving through the population in search of a vacant home range.

Transients

Resident Females

Resident Males

Transients

Dependent Kittens

Sources: Lindzey 1987, Lynch 1989.

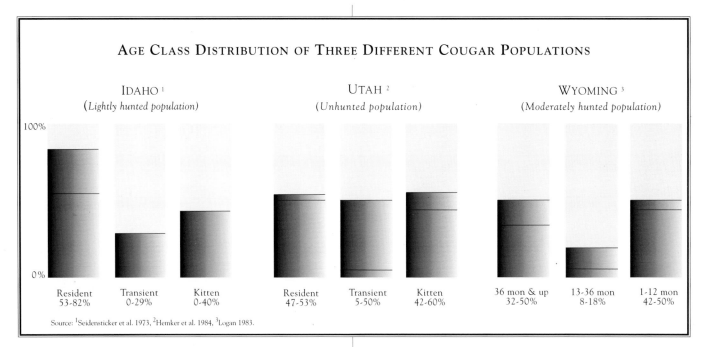

AGE CLASS DISTRIBUTION OF THREE DIFFERENT COUGAR POPULATIONS

IDAHO [1]	UTAH [2]	WYOMING [3]
(*Lightly hunted population*)	(*Unhunted population*)	(*Moderately hunted population*)

| Resident 53-82% | Transient 0-29% | Kitten 0-40% | Resident 47-53% | Transient 5-50% | Kitten 42-60% | 36 mon & up 32-50% | 13-36 mon 8-18% | 1-12 mon 42-50% |

Source: [1]Seidensticker et al. 1973, [2]Hemker et al. 1984, [3]Logan 1983.

by the fact that young transient cats are constantly on the move.[12] These factors, if not accounted for, can distort population estimates made by wildlife biologists.

Resident females generally outnumber resident males in a population.[25,32,33] This may be because females require smaller home ranges that frequently overlap those of other female cougars. Females also seem generally more tolerant of adjacent females and, as a result, more females can concentrate in a smaller area. Resident males, on the other hand, require larger home ranges that rarely overlap, and they tend to be intolerant of other males and are more widely scattered than resident females.

Young transient cougars usually leave their mother's home range (disperse) sometime during their second year. The newly independent cats occasionally linger in the birth area, while others leave immediately. They may wander for more than a year before establishing their own

home range.[22] If sufficient space is available, however, some females will remain in their birth areas; one young female in Nevada stayed in the mountain range of her birth, bred at 24 months, and established a home range adjacent to her mother's.[26] Female transients have even been known to take over their mother's home range after her death.[18]

Males tend to wander farther than females,[26] although how far either gender travels seems to vary. Transient males in the Diablo Mountains of California traveled up to 35 miles from their areas of birth.[16] In one Nevada population, males covered an average of 31 miles, while females averaged 18 miles.[26] One young cougar marked in the Bighorn Mountains of Wyoming appeared in northern Colorado, 300 miles from the original location.[34]

Transient males and females, seldom remain in one location longer than six months. How the cats "test" a population for vacated home ranges is poorly understood. It is generally thought that a transient either finds a vacant home range or displaces an older resident. If a vacant home range is found, the young male or female will settle down to the business of establishing its place in the population. If the population density is so high that no vacant home areas exist, the transient moves on.

Kenney Logan believes male transients enter a new population and for a period of time, make kills, avoid other lions, and avoid scraping. If they think they can establish a home range they begin to scrape. Meanwhile, the resident male, closely monitoring its home range, is busy investigating the newcomer's scrapes and kills. If the resident and newcomer encounter each other they may fight. As a result, the resident may kill the newcomer, the newcomer may kill the resident, or the newcomer may drive off or displace the resident.[17]

The role of transients in populations is important because they are the primary source of replacements for resident cougars who die as a result of hunting, old age, or accidents. Transients also ensure genetic mixing between populations,[12] and appear to be a major factor in the recovery of hunted populations. Cougar populations in isolated mountain ranges, such as those common to the Great

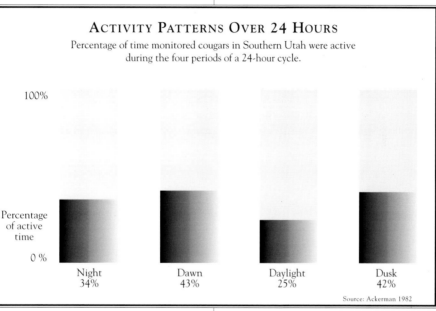

ACTIVITY PATTERNS OVER 24 HOURS

Percentage of time monitored cougars in Southern Utah were active during the four periods of a 24-hour cycle.

100%

Percentage of active time

0 %

| Night 34% | Dawn 43% | Daylight 25% | Dusk 42% |

Source: Ackerman 1982

Basin, are particularly vulnerable because immigration of transients is low.[35]

For example, aggressive predator control efforts wiped out all cougars in and around Yellowstone National Park by the 1920s, and—except for a few transients passing through—no cougars lived there for almost 50 years. But transients seem to be slowly recolonizing the 2.2 million-acre park; research biologist Kerry Murphy directs a field study of cougars in the region and estimates 14 to 17 resident mountain lions are now present. Radio collars have been attached to 9 females and 7 males, and the population produced 21 kittens in 1991. The region has abundant deer and elk, and the cougar population is increasing.[36]

As mentioned earlier, the availability of good hunting sites and prey numbers limit the number of cougars in an area. But birth, death, emigration, and immigration are all factors that greatly influence cougar population maintenance and growth. In the absence of hunting by humans, cougar populations will remain relatively constant.[12] Rick Hopkins found that the unhunted cougar population in the Diablo Mountains of California was relatively stable with a low turnover of residents.[16]

COUGARS ON THE MOVE

There is nothing more distinctive about cats than the way they move, and mountain lions are no different. The big cats are the epitome of graceful, lithe motion. Stealthy shadows that do not move so much as flow across the landscape.

"Consider the effect of broken terrain on prey," explains Kenney Logan. "Mountain lions are ballerinas at getting across broken terrain—steep slopes, boulders, outcroppings, and undercut ledges." Mule deer and elk are not as good at negotiating such rugged landscapes.[17] Here the cougar uses both cover and superior agility to its advantage, and employs yet another weapon in its predatory arsenal—it hunts under cover of darkness.

Cougars are not strictly nocturnal, as many once thought. Rather, they tend to be active at the same time as their prey, and deer tend to be active at dawn, dusk, and at night. Animals that are active during the twilight of dawn and dusk are said to be *crepuscular*. The big cat's excellent night vision makes it well suited for stalking during these low light periods. Florida panthers appear to be more active at sunrise and sunset,[37] and Paul Beier reports that in southern California mountain lions are active throughout the night.[39] During the winter in Idaho, radio-collared cougars were found to be more active at night (40 percent of the time they were located) than during daylight hours (14 percent of the time they were located). Daytime activity increased during the summer with an increased abundance of ground squirrels.[9] Bruce Ackerman studied cougar activity patterns in southern Utah and found the cats most active at sunrise and sunset, but less so during the winter. He also found that single adults were more active than females with young, but that the females became more active as their kittens grew.[3]

Most mule deer herds in mountainous areas of western North America migrate to lower elevations in the winter to avoid heavy snow and then come back to higher elevations in the summer. Predictably, cougars also shift their home-range use to follow these seasonal movements.[25] This elevational movement of cats following deer herds has been observed in Arizona, Idaho, California, and Nevada; in Idaho, cougars' winter home ranges were smaller than summer home ranges.[9, 25] Biologist Dave Ashman and his co-workers documented a case in Nevada where a male cougar occupied one mountain range in winter, then crossed 10 miles of flat, open desert to take up summer residence in another mountain range. Elsewhere in the state, cougars followed deer herds to lower elevations or traditional wintering grounds. During the cold Nevada winters, cougars avoided the north-facing slopes and frequented the south-facing slopes where there was less snow and more deer. When summer arrived, the cat shifted to the cooler north-facing slope, where there was more vegetation. Cougars also tended to restrict their movements to between 6,500 and 8,500 feet, where vegetation, deer, and other prey were most plentiful.[26]

Paul Beier has monitored some lions continuously for 24-hour periods to better understand their movements. He found that the lions in his California study area travel at a steady speed of approximately one-half mile per hour. Though there is a lot of variation, the cats seem to follow a cycle of traveling for a little less than an hour, followed by 30 minutes of rest.[38]

Mountain lions can cover a lot of ground in their nightly wanderings; a lion in the San Andres Mountains of New Mexico has been documented at 10 miles in a night.[17] Not surprisingly, Hemker and his coworkers found in their Utah study area that females with kittens less than six months old moved significantly shorter distances than females with older kittens, females without kittens, transients, or resident males. One resident male traveled eight miles in a one-day period, but this represents only the straight-line distance between locations on a map and does not reflect the actual distance covered.[25] Here is why.

Cougars have two basic patterns of movement: hunting and traveling. When the big cat is looking for prey, it traverses a zigzag course through it home range. An entire day of searching for prey likely brings the cougar only a few linear miles from its starting point. The cat is basically searching and has no specific destination in mind. A traveling cat, with a specific destination in mind is a different matter.

The route will be more direct, though it will still take advantage of the landscape, following ridges, major drainages, or using low passes.[22]

A common myth about the daily movements of cougars is that they follow a regular and predictable circuit around their home range. This assumption may stem partly from observations of domestic cats or vague attempts to

apply human behavior to cougars. A variety of studies that monitored cougar movements with radio telemetry found no such patterns. Cougars move freely and arbitrarily about their home ranges and have never been seen to pass a fixed location at set intervals.[22] As a stalking predator that depends on the element of surprise to capture its prey, regularity of movement would handicap the cougar's ability to survive.

CHAPTER 3. COUGARS AT HOME (NOTES)

1. Dassman, R.F. 1981. *Wildlife biology*, 2nd edition. John Wiley and Sons, New York.

2. Dixon, K.R. 1982. Mountain lion. Pages 711–727 *in* J.A. Chapman and G.A. Feldhamer, eds. *Wild mammals of North America.* John Hopkins University Press. Baltimore.

3. Ackerman, B.B. 1982. Cougar predation and ecological energetics in southern Utah. M.S. thesis, Utah State University, Logan.

4. Lindzey, F.G., B.B. Ackerman, D. Barnhurst, T. Becker, T.P. Hemker, S.P. Laing, C. Mecham, and W.D. Van Sickle. 1989. *Boulder-Escalante cougar project final report.* Utah Division of Wildlife Resources, Salt Lake City, Utah.

5. Wallmo, O.C. 1978. Mule and black-tailed deer. Pages 30–41 *in* J.L. Schmidt and D.L. Gilbert, eds. *Big game of North America: Ecology and management.* Wildlife Management Institute. Stackpole Books.

6. Mills, J. 1990. Deer old game. *National Wildlife*, October–November 1990: 59.

7. Laing, S.P. 1988. Cougar habitat selection and spatial use patterns in southern Utah. M.S. thesis. University of Wyoming, Laramie.

8. Hornocker, M.G. 1969a. Winter territoriality in mountain lions. *Journal of Wildlife Management,* 33:457–464.

9. Seidensticker, J.C., IV, M.G. Hornocker, W.V. Wiles, and J.P. Messick. 1973. Mountain lion social organization in the Idaho Primitive Area. *Wildlife Monographs,* 35.

10. Logan, K.A and L.L. Irwin. 1985. Mountain lion habitats in the Big Horn Mountains, Wyoming. *Wildlife Society Bulletin* 13: 257–262.

11. Shaw, H.G. 1991. Wildlife Biologist, General Wildlife Services, Chino Valley, Arizona. (Personal communication)

12. Lindzey, F. 1987. Mountain lion. Pages 656–668 *in* M. Novak, J.A. Baker, M.E. Obbard, and B. Malloch, eds. *Wild furbearer management and conservation in North America.* Ministry of Natural Resources, Ontario, Canada.

13. Lopez, B. 1981. The elusive mountain lion. *GEO* June: 98–116.

14. Bass, O.L. 1991. Wildlife Biologist, Everglades National Park Research Center, Homestead, Florida. (Personal communication)

15. Kitchener, A. 1991. *The natural history of the wild cats.* Cornell University Press. Ithaca, New York.

16. Hopkins, R.A. 1989. Ecology of the puma in the Diablo Range, California. Ph.D. dissertation, University of California at Berkeley.

17. Logan, K.A. 1991. Wildlife Research Institute, Inc., Moscow, Idaho. (Personal communication)

18. Lindzey, F.G. 1991. Wildlife Biologist, U.S. Fish and Wildlife Service, Wyoming Cooperative Fish and Wildlife Research Unit, University of Wyoming, Laramie, Wyoming. (Personal communication)

19. Kiltie, R.A. 1991. How cats work. Pages 54–67 *in* J. Seidensticker and S. Lumpkin, eds. *Great cats: Majestic creatures of the wild.* Rodale Press, Emmaus, Pennsylvania.

20. Mellen, J. 1991. Cat behavior. Pages 68–75 *in* J. Seidensticker and S. Lumpkin, eds. *Great cats: Majestic creatures of the wild.* Rodale Press, Emmaus, Pennsylvania.

21. Hornocker, M.G. 1970. An analysis of mountain lion predation upon mule deer and elk in the Idaho Primative Area. *Wildlife Monographs.* 21:1–39.

22. Shaw, H.G. 1989. *Soul among lions.* Johnson Books. Boulder, Colorado.

23. Lynch, W. 1989. The elusive cougar. *Canadian Geographic* August/September: 24–31.

24. Sitton, L.W. and S. Wallen. 1976. *California mountain lion study.* California Department of Fish and Game. Sacramento.

25. Hemker, T.P., F.G. Lindzey, and B.B. Ackerman. 1984. Population characteristics and movement patterns of cougars in southern Utah. *Journal of Wildlife Management,* 48(4):1275–1284.

26. Ashman, D., G.C. Christensen, M.L. Hess, G.K. Tsukamoto, and M.S. Wickersham. 1983. *The mountain lion in Nevada.* Nevada Department of Wildlife, Reno.

27. Hopkins, R.A. 1991. Wildlife Biologist, H.T. Harvey and Associates, Alviso, California. (Personal communication)

28. Pall, O., M. Jalkotzy, and I. Ross. 1988. *The cougar in Alberta.* Fish and Wildlife Division. Alberta Forestry, Lands and Wildlife. Associated Resource Consultants. Calgary, Alberta.

29. Sweanor, L.L. 1990. Mountain lion social organization in a desert environment. M.S. thesis, University of Idaho, Moscow.

30. de Treville, S. 1991. Wildlife Biologist. de Treville Environmental Engineering. San Diego, California. (Personal communication)

31. Shaw, H. 1987. *Mountain lion field guide.* 3rd Edition. Special Report Number 9. Arizona Game and Fish Department.

32. Anderson, A.E. 1983. A *critical review of literature on puma (Felis concolor).* Colorado Division of Wildlife. Special Report Number 54.

33. Logan, K.A. 1983. Mountain lion population and habitat characteristics in the Big Horn Mountains of Wyoming. M.S. thesis, University of Wyoming, Laramie.

34. Parfit, M. 1985. Its days as a varmint are over, but the cougar is still on the run. *Smithsonian,* November: 68–79.

35. Ackerman, B.B., F.G. Lindzey, and T.P. Hemker. 1984. Cougar food habits in southern Utah. *Journal of Wildlife Management,* 48:147–155.

36. Murphy, K. 1991. Wildlife Biologist. Wildlife Research Institute, Inc., Moscow, Idaho. (Personal communication)

37. Maehr, D.S., E.D. Land, J.C. Roof, and J.W. McCown. 1990c. Day beds, natal dens, and activity of Florida panthers. *Proceedings of the annual conference of southeast fish and wildlife agencies,* 44: In press.

38. Beier, P. 1992. Project Leader, Orange County Cooperative Mountain Lion Study, Department of Forestry and Resource Management, University of California, Berkeley. (Personal communication)

AN ALMOST-PERFECT PREDATOR

ANATOMY OF A HUNTER

Thirty-five million years of evolution have honed *Felis concolor* into an almost perfect predator. The cougar's keen senses, muscular body, and remarkable adaptability make it ideally suited for a predatory existence. Because they are the most exclusive of meat-eaters, almost every feature of a cat's body is related to the way it detects and catches its prey.[1]

DETECTING PREY

The big cats use all of their senses in their ongoing search for prey. When the Florida panther stepped in front of my truck that night in the Everglades, and the eerie glint of its eyes flashed back at me, I was witness to a universal feature of feline legend. But the eyes of a cat are not windows to the fires of Hell, as witch hunters in the Middle Ages believed;[2] they are actually the marvelous adaptation of a nocturnal hunter.

Cats have extraordinary vision. The eyeball, pupil, and lens are proportionately larger than other carnivores. The eyes of a domestic cat are only slightly smaller than those of humans, but the cat can open its pupil to a maximum area three times larger than humanscan;[3] this increases light-gathering ability and enhances night vision. Cougars are both nocturnal and crepuscular (active during the twilight hours of dawn and dusk). As a result, their eyes are proportionately smaller than the mostly nocturnal lynx, making pumas suited to hunting both in daylight and at night.[4,5] The amount of light entering the eyeball is controlled by the pupil, and the pupil in smaller cats is elliptical. This allows it to open as wide as possible at night, but close almost completely in bright light, protecting light-sensitive cells. Cougars and other big cats have round or oval pupils, reflecting a somewhat lesser dependency on nocturnal hunting.[1,3]

After passing through the pupil and lens, light strikes a layer of light-sensitive cells at the back of the eye called the retina. There are two kinds of light receptor cells in the retinas of mammals: rods and cones. Rods function in low levels of light and do not detect color, while cones are sensitive to high levels of light and are used in color vision. Not surprisingly, the eyes of cats consist primarily of rods, though there is a concentration of cones near the center of the retina as in our own eyes. There is evidence that cats can only discern the color of relatively close or large objects, but much remains to be learned about color vision in cats.[3]

Behind the retina is a thin layer of reflective cells called a *tapetum lucidum*, meaning "bright carpet." The tapetum reflects light back through the rods and further enhances interpretation of low-light images, giving the cougar a second chance to discern what it is looking at. The tapetum is responsible for the characteristic "eye-shine" of reflected light that is frequently seen in mammals at night.[1,2,6] It was the Florida panther's tapetum I saw that night in the Everglades.

Another characteristic of feline vision is that the eyes are close together and facing forward. This allows the field of vision of the two eyes to overlap, resulting in binocular vision. Binocular vision provides excellent depth perception and the ability to precisely judge distance; cats have the most highly developed binocular vision of all carnivores.[1] The cat's total visual field spans 287 degrees, with a binocular overlap of 130 degrees. Humans, by contrast, have a binocular overlap of 120 degrees in a total visual field of 200 degrees. The cougar's depth perception is most sensitive within a range of 50 to 80 feet, a critical adaptation for a predator that stalks its prey and attacks from a short distance.[6]

While a cougar's extraordinary vision seems to give it

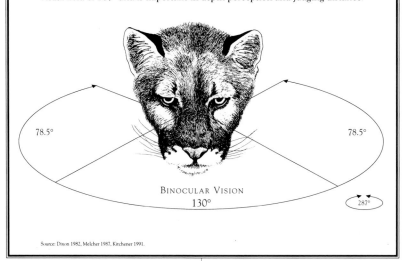

TOTAL VISUAL FIELD OF COUGARS

Like all cats, the eyes of a cougar are directed forward in their skull, resulting in an overlap of the visual field of the two eyes. Binocular vision covers 130° in a total visual field of 287° and is important in depth perception and judging distance.

78.5°   78.5°

BINOCULAR VISION
130°

287°

Source: Dixon 1982, Melcher 1987, Kitchener 1991.

a distinct advantage over its prey, nature has a way of compensating for advantages. In humans, the high concentration of cones in our eyes allows us to resolve (discern) visual detail in daylight, while the low concentration of rods inhibits our ability to resolve detail in low light. This resolving power is called visual acuity. While the concentration of rods and the presence of a tapetum has increased the cat's sensitivity to low light, it has sacrificed visual acuity. Rods do not allow for much discrimination between light wavelengths, and the tapetum further blurs the image the cat sees. As a result, cats' vision at night is six times better than that of humans, but humans have better visual acuity.[1,2,3]

Further, in prey species such as deer, the eyes are mounted on the side of their head. This arrangement does not allow binocular vision but does increase the total field of view and the ability to detect predators.[7] Cats also have a heightened sensitivity to movement, and biologists believe that it is the movment of prey that triggers the puma to attack. This may explain why prey typically will "freeze" after detecting a predator.[6] In the world of predator and prey, there seems to be a defense for every offense.

Although little research has been done on hearing in cougars, it is known that domestic cats can detect their prey by sound as well as sight. They can hear frequencies in the ultrasonic range and are able to move their small, rounded ears together or independently to isolate these sounds. It is also believed that an enlarged auditory bullae (the portion of the skull surrounding the middle ear) may enhance a cat's sensitivity to certain sounds.[1,3,8]

Experts speculate that in most cats, vision and hearing are important for hunting, while smell plays a more active role in social behavior.[3] In the previous chapter it was explained that pumas have a special olfactory organ in the roof of their mouth that is employed during a flehman response, presumably to determine the reproductive condition of a female.[11] Cougars also seem to share their domestic cousin's attraction to catnip.[8,12] Smell, a well-developed feline sense, is not primarily used in hunting. However, "We probably underestimate how much cougars use their sense of smell," says Fred Lindzey, "I once saw a captive male picking up the scent of a deer." Lindzey thinks cougars probably do not use their sense of smell in hunting, but can generally use it to determine whether deer are in the area.[9] Bogue and Ferrari observed a six-month-old puma kitten follow a scent trail they laid down through undergrowth with a piece of hide from a freshly killed deer.[10] Nonetheless, dogs' sense of smell is much more highly developed. The longer muzzle of a dog boasts almost 50 square inches of olfactory cells to the cat's 6 square inches, and 5 percent of canine brain volume is committed to its sense of smell, compared to 3 percent in cats.[1]

Cats have an acute sense of touch, particularly with the tip of their nose, toes, and paws.[8] A cat's whiskers are specially adapted as tactile sensors; during prey capture they are extended like a net in front of the mouth so the cat can determine exactly where the prey is to accurately inflict the killing bite.[13] Barry Lopez tells of one biologist who believes that a cougar's paws are so sensitive that when it attacks deer in pitch black it can determine the location of the head by instantly sensing the direction its hair is growing.[14]

CAPTURING PREY

A mountain lion is the personification of power, grace, strength, speed, and agility, largely due to heavy musculature attached to a light but strong skeleton. The majority of a cougar's body weight is muscle and sinew, with only a relatively small portion made up of bone and organs. Long, muscular legs and a flexible backbone allow strong extended strides, while its long, heavy tail provides balance on quick turns and uneven ground.[15] Horizontal leaps of 45 feet have been recorded, along with vertical leaps of 15 feet. This ability may be partly due to the fact that the cat's rear legs are longer than its front legs. An adaption for jumping is a valuable characteristic both for attacking prey and moving through the rugged terrain most cougars inhabit.[8] Further, the anatomy of a cougar's front limbs allows the animal to pivot sharply without losing lateral traction,[14] an important feature when grasping large prey at high speed.

The big cat is built for speed, not endurance. Writer Jim Bob Tinsley relates that, "It [the cougar] can easily outrun a pack of dogs for a few hundred yards, but its small lungs limit the distance it can cover at full stride. When out of breath, it must seek the temporary shelter of a tree or some other natural protection."[16] Ralph Schmidt, who works with Alberta lion researchers Martin Jalkotsy and Ian Ross, believes cougars are the fastest predator in North America. "I've seen cougars jump out of trees and run up a slope at an unbelievable rate of speed," says Schmidt, with a pronounced tone of respect.[17] Apparently no cougar has ever submitted to the stopwatch, but it is telling to consider that in some parts of the western United States, cougars have been known to occasionally kill pronghorn (*Antilocapra americana*), the fastest land animal in North America.[16,18]

Cats and many other carnivores walk upright on their toes, a stance known as digitigrade, as opposed to the plantigrade stance found in humans and bears.[3] Webbed

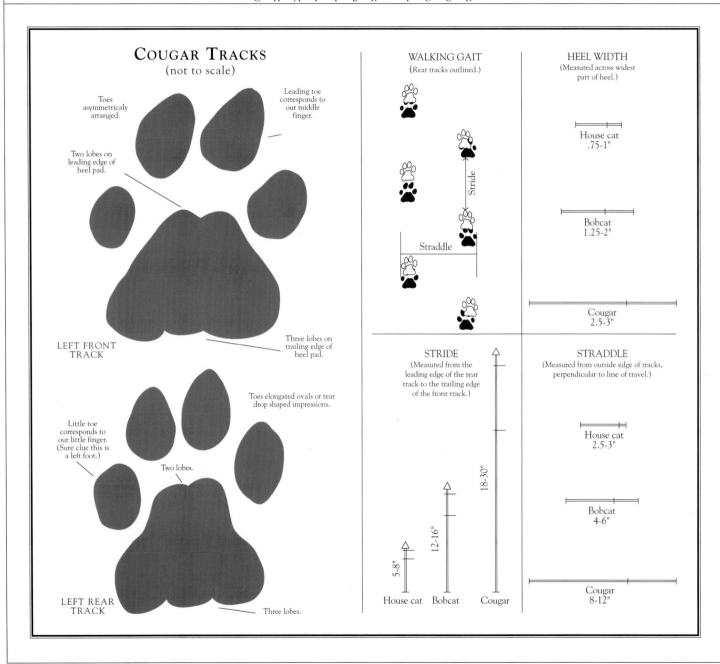

COUGAR TRACKS
(not to scale)

Toes asymmetricaly arranged.

Leading toe corresponds to our middle finger.

Two lobes on leading edge of heel pad.

Three lobes on trailing edge of heel pad.

LEFT FRONT TRACK

Toes elongated ovals or tear drop shaped impressions.

Little toe corresponds to our little finger. (Sure clue this is a left foot.)

Two lobes.

Three lobes.

LEFT REAR TRACK

WALKING GAIT
(Rear tracks outlined.)

Stride

Straddle

HEEL WIDTH
(Measured across widest part of heel.)

House cat
.75-1"

Bobcat
1.25-2"

Cougar
2.5-3"

STRIDE
(Measured from the leading edge of the rear track to the trailing edge of the front track.)

5-8"

12-16"

18-30"

House cat   Bobcat   Cougar

STRADDLE
(Measured from outside edge of tracks, perpendicular to line of travel.)

House cat
2.5-3"

Bobcat
4-6"

Cougar
8-12"

Cougar Tracks

by Susan C. Morse

1. Upon first investigating a track or tracks, step back and examine the "style" of the track sequences. By process of elimination, the tracker can usually begin to discern what the tracks probably are by identifying specific features which are either diagnostic of wild cats or domestic or wild canids. (For a more detailed description of these features, see *Mountain Lion Field Guide* by Harley G. Shaw, Third Edition, Special Report No. 9, Arizona Game and Fish Department.)

2. Dog tracks usually register (show) the animal's forward moving "style" of locomotion. Coyotes and wolves and even their domestic counterparts *usually* trot, and often, gallop in order to get around. The result is very diagnostic, for the heel pad will shove up the surface material into a *ridge* on the top edge of the heel.

3. Cats usually walk through life; like their domestic cousins, they choose a very easy and deliberate walking pace with the result that their tracks typically appear clean and undisturbed, with the animal's weight showing in an evenly distributed impression.

4. Don't assume that a track automatically belongs to a dog if it has nail marks showing. Some sheep dogs and hounds have nails which are very worn with the result that they occasionally won't show at all, whereas cougars and bobcats will occasionally use their claws for extra traction while walking upon slippery or disagreeable surfaces. The difference in what we *see* is significant — cat claw marks appear as sharply defined slits in contrast to the blunt impressions of canid nails.

5. Upon further examination of a track, look for the following features: Cougar tracks feature the typical cat heel imprint, which has two lobes on the top (or leading edge) of the heel and three lobes at the base (or bottom) of the heel. Be aware that some guidebooks do not always show the diagnostic two lobes on the leading edge, while others do. Both are correct for these features may or may not appear, depending on the properties of the surface upon which the lion is walking, and the corresponding depth of his foot impressions. Most often, however, the three lobe pattern at the base of the heel will show.

6. The toes of a cougar track are asymmetrically arranged and appear as elongated ovals or tear drop shaped impressions. The leading toe corresponds to our middle finger, with the little toe (like our little finger) providing the sure clue as to whether it is a right or left foot we are examining.

7. Walking track sequences of the mountain lion usually involves a *direct register* of tracks, if the animal is stalking or walking upon snow or a muddy surface. This means the left and right hind feet have been placed directly in the corresponding impressions made by the front feet. By contrast, an over-stepped register or slightly offset direct register occurs if the animal is walking normally. The hind foot is placed on top of or forward of the fore foot impression.

8. The cougar's trail will appear as a neat, regular placement of paired or overlapped footprints, in which the left and right hind feet have been placed in or near the corresponding impressions made by the front feet. Note that unless cougars are actually stalking, playing or running away from an enemy, their trails rarely depict variations in gait.

skin and fur between the toes muffle sound as the cat walks, and while stalking or walking on snow or a muddy surface, the hindfeet can be placed almost exactly in the track of the forefeet.[20] Cougar tracks reveal four toe pads in front of a smooth, calloused, three-lobed heel pad. Adult tracks average 3 1/2 inches in width and length,[19] with the fore-paws usually larger than the hindpaws. During normal walking the claws are retracted, but during quick accelera-tion they are extended and used for traction.[8]

Sharp claws are important for seizing and controlling prey so the cougar can deliver the killing neck bite. To keep their claws sharp, cougars have spring-like ligaments that keep the claws retracted inside fleshy sheaths and ele-vated above the ground most of the time. Retraction of the claws is passive, requiring no effort on the part of the cat. In use, the muscles in the forelegs contract, which in turn protract the claws, and the cougar is ready for action. As Kiltie has noted, it probably makes more sense to call them "protractile" claws.[3]

The skull is short and round, with 16 teeth in the upper jaw and 14 in the lower jaw[6]. Cougars have a powerful bite because of the reduced length of their jaws and their large jaw-closing muscles, the *temporalis* and *masseter*. Atop its skull, the cat has a bony ridge called the sagittal crest,

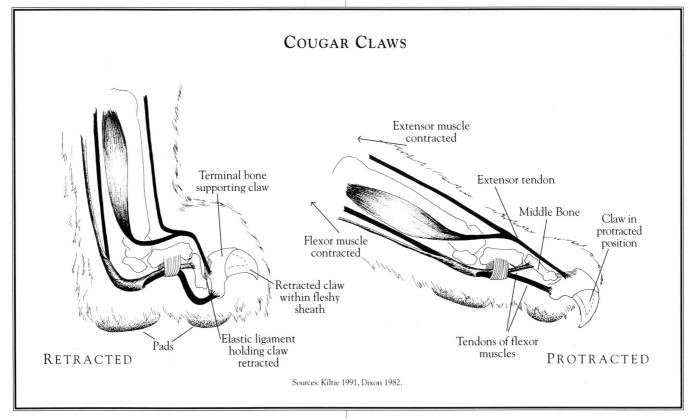

COUGAR CLAWS

Terminal bone
supporting claw

Retracted claw
within fleshy
sheath

Pads

Elastic ligament
holding claw
retracted

RETRACTED

Extensor muscle
contracted

Extensor tendon

Middle Bone

Claw in
protracted
position

Flexor muscle
contracted

Tendons of flexor
muscles

PROTRACTED

Sources: Kiltie 1991, Dixon 1982.

rion, as well as other carnivores, such as bobcats, coyotes, and other cougars.[18,32]

The puma's dependence on smaller prey is more pronounced in South America. In Chile's Torres del Paine National Park, pumas subsist primarily on European hares (*Lepus europaeus*), followed by guanacos (*Lama guanicoe*) and domestic sheep (Yanez et al. 1986). Biologist Louise Emmons found that pumas in the jungles of Peru preyed on small rodents, oppossums, bats, and lizards. The majority of their prey were agoutis and pacas, rodents weighing 2 to 22 pounds.[34] The big cats are able to kill and eat most animals in their home range.

When the abundance of their primary prey declines, cougars have been known to switch their diet. This occur-

red in Big Bend National Park in western Texas, where cougars and male bobcats usually feed on deer. When the mule deer population crashed in 1980–1981, both cats were forced to switch to peccaries and lagomorphs (rabbits and hares), the next largest prey.[35]

The diet of a cougar also varies according to its sex and age. Solitary cats seem to consume more small prey than do females with young, while transients likely focus their efforts on smaller prey until they develop the skills to hunt and kill larger prey. Females must feed young for up to 18 months, so killing large animals is a more efficient way to procure a lot of fresh meat quickly. Bruce Ackerman and his colleagues concluded that, considering the food requirements of females with young, breeding populations

PREY ITEMS REPORTED TAKEN BY COUGARS

LARGE WILD ANIMALS		SMALL WILD ANIMALS		DOMESTIC ANIMALS	OTHER ITEMS
Mule deer	Bear	Snowshoe hare	White-footed mouse	Sheep	Turkey
White-tailed deer	Bobcat	Other rabbits	Meadow vole	Cattle	Ruffled grouse
Elk	Cougar	Pika	Raccoon	Horse	Fish
Bighorn sheep	Coyote	Marmot	Fox	Burro	Insects
Moose	Pampas deer	Skunk	Coatamundi	Goat	Grass
Mountain goat	Huemul	Ground squirrels	Agouti	Pig	Berries
Pronghorn	Guanaco	Pine squirrel	Brocket	Dog	Rhea
Peccary	Wild boar	Flying Squirerel	Opposum	Cat	
Porcupine		Rock Squirrel		Chicken	
Beaver		Pocket Gopher		Peafowl	
Badger		Woodrat			
Armadillo		Cotton Rat			

Source: Young & Goldman 1946; Spalding and Lesowski 1971; Russell 1978; Currier 1983.

of cougars could not exist in areas devoid of large prey like deer.[36]

How often a cougar kills a deer depends on a variety of factors:

~ Sex and reproductive status
~ Size of the dependent young
~ Social status
~ Abundance of alternate prey
~ Rate of spoilage of kill
~ Time of year

Estimated frequencies of kill vary from 1 deer per 10 to 14 days[27] to 1 deer per 2 to 3 days.[36] As stated previously, females with dependent kittens require greater quantities of meat, quantities that increase as the kittens grow. Ackerman estimated the following kill rates for a resident female in southern Utah:

Solitary resident female	1 deer per 16 days
Resident female with three 3-month-old kittens	1 deer per 9 days
Resident female with three 15-month-old kittens[37]	1 deer per 3 days

Having evolved as an opportunistic predator, that may go without eating for days at a time, cougars exhibit fast-and-gorge feeding behavior. Captive cougars will eat 5 to 12 pounds of meat per day, more after deprivation, which is typical of this behavior.[25] Sensitive to spoilage, cougars seem to prefer their meat fresh, though they have been known to eat carrion when near starvation. In the warm temperatures of Arizona, spoilage of the carcass will typically restrict a cougar's use of a kill to no more than four days.[38] Kills can be fed on for longer periods in more tem-perate regions. This is a decided advantage during cold winters when metabolic demands are high. One researcher in Idaho observed a cougar remain with an elk carcass for 19 days during one particularly cold winter.[31]

After killing a deer, a cougar goes about its feeding with almost surgical precision. The cat plucks the fur from the point of incision using its teeth, then, using its claws, the flank is opened behind the ribs. The stomach and in-testines are pulled out and dragged away from the carcass; heart, lungs, and liver are removed and eaten first.[6,38] These organs contain higher concentrations of protein, fat, and vitamins than does muscle tissue. The liver in particular contains a high proportion of vitamins, amino acids, and glycogen, the primary source of metabolic energy. The fact these organs are consumed first is an important characteris-tic of the cougar's fast-and-gorge feeding behavior. It may be a survival adaptation in case continued feeding is not possible;[39] a young transient cougar risks losing its kill to a resident lion, so the transient may gorge then leave the vicinity of the kill.[40] When continued feedings are possi-ble, they include the rear quarters, then muscle tissue on the inside of the legs. If it's been a long time since the last meal, the lion will feed heavily, consuming up to ten pounds of meat.[38] Generally left uneaten are the head, large bones, hide, and digestive tract. A solitary cougar can consume 75 percent of a carcass by weight,[39] while a female with kittens will perform an even more thorough job of consumption.[38]

Because they feed on more easily digestible meat than all other carnivores, cats have relatively short digestive tracts. Both the small and large intestine are shorter and less efficient than in the more omnivorous dog. It is known, for example, that domestic cats have a mean digestive effi-ciency for total energy of 79 percent, compared with 89 percent for the domestic dog.[1] While the physiology of cougar digestion is poorly understood, the cat seems to sur-vive on a diet rich in protein and fat. Veterinarian Melody

Roelke reports that Florida panthers generally pass all food matter within 36 hours.[41] Houston has suggested that since the hunting behavior of cats requires quick acceleration, they minimize body weight and inertia by having a short, light gut.[42] Unlike dogs, cats appear to be unable to tolerate low levels of nitrogen (from protein) in their diets.[3]

Little is known about the water requirements of pumas. Stanley Young observed that "When water is scarce the puma apparently is capable of existing for long periods without it. This seems particularly evident in some of the dry semi-desert areas of southwestern Utah."[12] Kitchener believes that although cats have access to free water, part of their liquid requirement probably comes from their prey.[1] Kenney Logan agrees. "There is no doubt cougars drink free water. They visit springs and guzzlers (man-made water catchments). They probably get a lot of water from drinking the blood of prey. We find very little blood spillage in the kills on our study area." Logan believes blood provides the cougar with nutrients, vitamins, and water.[43]

PREDATORY BEHAVIOR

Cougars are ambush predators.[44] Like most cats, with the notable exception of the cheetah, they attempt to catch their prey unaware, rather than chase it down. Unlike a bear, which kills its prey through brute force, the cougar is the epitome of speed and precision. The cat is silent on approach, quick on the attack, and efficient in making the kill.[15,38]

Few people have ever seen a mountain lion make a kill in the wild and a great deal of myth surrounds how it is done.[38] Stories of cougars killing 800-pound steers and scaling 10-foot fences with the unfortunate bovine still clutched in its jaws originated in frontier imaginations rather than any documented incident. Paul Leyhausen has done extensive research on predatory behavior in domestic and wild cats, including pumas.[13] It is now believed that prey-capture behavior is very similar in all species of wild cats.[1] In cougars, the process begins with the hunt.

The cougar is a relentless hunter. The search for prey is driven by the cat's hunger and, in the case of a female, the need to feed growing kittens. The hungrier the cat, the greater the tendency to roam, with effort focused on areas where prey was previously found.[13] The cougar navigates its home range in a zigzag course, skirting open areas and taking advantage of available cover.[31,38] The cat's keen senses are focused to pick up the slightest movement, odor, or sound. How frequently the cat encounters prey depends on the number of prey in its home range, the density of cover, and the cougar's searching behavior.[6] Once prey is detected, stalking begins.

ESTIMATED KILL RATE AND ANNUAL KILL BY COUGARS

ESTIMATED KILL RATE	ESTIMATED ANNUAL KILL
1 deer/7 days (single adult)	—
1 deer/3+days (female with cubs)[1]	—
1 deer/10 days and	—
1 porcupine/7.2 days[2]	—
1 deer/4-10 days[3]	—
1 deer/10-14 days[4]	14-20 deer (@ 140 lbs) or 5.7 elk (@ 385 lbs)
1 deer or calf/10.4 days (single female) or 1 deer or	17-25 deer (@ 112 lbs)
calf/6.8 days (female with cubs)[5]	10-14 calves (@ 200 lbs)
1 deer/8-16 days (single adult) or	52 deer
1 deer/2-3 days (female w/cubs)[6]	—

Source/Location: [1]Young and Goldman 1946/throughout western U.S.; [2]Connolly 1949/central Utah; [3]Robinette et al. 1959/Utah and Nevada; [4]Hornocker 1970/central Idaho; [5]Shaw 1977/central Arizona; [6]Ackerman 1982/southern Utah.

The cougar fixes its gaze on the animal, lowers itself to the ground in a crouch, and begins to maneuver closer to the animal, taking care to remain hidden. It assumes an alert watching posture: head is stretched forward, the whiskers spread wide, and ears erect and turned toward the front (illustrated on page 21). The cat will hold this position for minutes on end following the prey's slightest movement with its head.[13] When the prey draws within 50 feet or less, *Felis concolor* strikes.[38]

Flattened against the ground, the cat darts forward, either running or with several bounds, and quickly closes the distance to its prey.[13] The angle of attack is usually from the rear or side.[1] Once at its prey's side it grasps the neck and shoulders with the front paws, claws extended. It will frequently strike its prey with such force during the final charge that in the case of a large animal such as deer or elk, the prey will be knocked off their feet. Although cats will attack from elevated positions such as a tree or boulder, they almost never land directly on their prey. To do so would provide a very unstable landing area and a poor platform from which to counter the unpredictable movements of its prey. When attacking large prey, it is important for

the puma to keep its weight on its hind legs so that it can adjust its position to maintain control, or if necessary, to make a prudent retreat to avoid injury.[13] (It has already been noted that cougars are occasionally injured and even killed during such attacks.) Instead the cat lands on the ground short of the prey and attacks from there.[13]

The prey is normally killed with a bite to the back of the neck at the base of the skull (illustrated on page 37). The large canines are inserted between the vertebrae like a wedge, forcing the vertebrae apart and breaking the spinal cord.[13] The speed with which this takes place indicates that the concentration of nerves in its canines allows the cat to "feel" its way to the vertebrae in a fraction of a second.[5] In the case of larger prey such as elk, the neck may be broken by pulling the head down and back, breaking it directly or in a fall.[45] If this fails the cougar may grasp the throat, crushing the windpipe. This necessitates death through asphyxiation and takes longer, exposing the cougar to possible injury.[6,38] The efficiency of the kill will vary, depending on prey size, cougar size, angle of attack, and other circumstances. Hornocker found that cougars were successful 82 percent of the time in attacks on mule deer and elk in the Idaho Primitive Area.[27]

Following a successful kill, cats rarely feed immediately.[13] This characteristic is probably a response to the level of hunger, energy expended during the attack, and the excitement of the attack. At some point, though, the cougar will drag or carry the carcass to a protected spot, such as under a tree, and begin to feed.[38]

The cougar's instinct to hide its kill is strong. After eating its fill, the cougar will hide the carcass by covering it with pine needles, limbs, and small twigs. Hiding the carcass protects it from scavengers, such as coyotes and ravens, and keeps the meat cool and fresh. Using its claws as rakes, the cat will stand over the kill and drag the debris inward with its front feet. Even soil and small rocks are used when nothing else is available. Shaw once found a deer killed on a large granite boulder in Arizona by a radio-collared lion. The female cougar had placed a single twig on the carcass before leaving.[38]

The cougar will typically remain in the vicinity of its kill for up to five days, making frequent trips back to feed and protect the carcass from other carnivores and scavengers. It's not uncommon for a lion to move the carcass after each feeding. Fred Lindzey reports that lions will sometimes move a carcass over 100 yards each time, then feed on it.[9] How long the cat remains with the kill and the degree to which it is consumed depends on the size and weight of the cougar, the size of the prey, and weather conditions.[38] It has already been noted that a female with kittens will consume the carcass more completely than a solitary cat.[39] What causes abandonment of a kill is unknown. Some are fed on only once, leaving much of the meat uneaten, others are devoured completely, including the bone marrow. Spoilage and disturbance of the carcass are the most likely causes. Whatever the reason, the cat will leave the immediate area and eventually begin the search for its next prey.

EFFECTS OF COUGAR PREDATION ON PREY

In nature, predation is the rule, not the exception. All animals compete for the resources their environment provides and there are few animals that are not subject to some kind of predation.[46] Prey populations are influenced by many factors, some of the more important being the availability of food, denning sites, disease, migration, emigration, and predators.[1] The specific impact predators have on prey populations is one of the least understood and most controversial areas of study in wildlife science. Because an in-depth discussion of predator/prey relations is beyond the scope of this book, the following section gives only a brief overview of the relationship between cougars and their prey.

Traditional thinking was that predators slaughtered everything in sight and were capable of decimating entire prey populations. It was believed that by eradicating the predators, the prey populations would rise, leaving more game for the human hunter. As a result, the Scottish wildcat was almost eradicated by the early 20th century, large predators in African game parks were "controlled" until recently,[1] and attempts were made to exterminate the mountain lion. The puma's occasional habit of killing livestock didn't help the situation.[6]

The next evolution in predatory/prey theory suggested that predators weed out old or sick individuals, thereby improving the health of the prey population.[1] This is sometimes referred to as *sanitation*. While the sanitation theory has elements of truth, it is frequently a distorted and oversimplified interpretation of Darwin's theory of natural selection.[38] Cougars are known to prey on both healthy and sick animals,[27] and whether the cat selects for unhealthy prey is generally considered unproven. Both healthy and weak are vulnerable because of the cat's ambush-hunting method.[25] Shaw has pointed out that some aspects of the lion's behavior suggest that they may actually tend to select for younger and more active animals—that lions are somehow triggered to attack active prey.[38]

Current thinking is that cougars select prey more at random; as opportunistic hunters they will kill what they can, sick or healthy, as the opportunity arises. While circumstance and opportunity seem to be more important that conscious selection on the part of the cat, studies indicate certain segments of the prey population appear to be more vulnerable than others.

Mountain lions were found to kill a greater proportion of mule deer fawns and mature bucks during studies in Colorado[47] and Nevada.[48] Hornocker observed the same pattern in lion-killed elk in Idaho.[27] The Boulder-Escalante cougar study in southern Utah revealed that adult males (all seasons), fawns (in winter), and older deer (7+ years) were most vulnerable to cougar predation.[37] Cougars in the Diablo Mountains of California appear to take more of a cross section of the deer population. The cats showed a preference for bucks over fawns, and did not appear to select for old and infirm.[44]

Bucks may be more vulnerable because they are more distracted during the mating season. They are in poor physical condition during the winter and have a tendency to winter at higher elevations and in broken terrain, the preferred habitat of the cougar. Unlike the more solitary bucks, females winter in loose groups, which increases their ability to detect predators. Should the group be attacked, the confusion of many fleeing animals reduces the cat's chance of success. The very young and very old are less vigorous and thus more vulnerable as a result.[6, 25] Other factors have been noted by research biologists. Ackerman believes mule deer vulnerability is determined by their behavior, such as group alertness, parental care, and differing habitat use.[37] Susan de Treville has suggested that in the brushy chaparral habitat of California, bucks with antlers may hesitate to "bust brush" for fear of getting hung up. Consequently, they were more frequently seen in the open.[49]

The effect of predators on prey populations is not always clear. "The question becomes not 'Do pumas limit or reduce prey growth rates?'" explains Rick Hopkins, "but 'When do they and under what circumstances?'" Hopkins points out that predator/prey interactions are very complex and depend on:

~ Prey numbers
~ Predator numbers
~ Prey characteristics
~ Predator characteristics
~ Abundance of alternative prey[50]

In the past, it was widely believed that large predators such as wolves and cougars held the numbers of deer, elk, and moose in check and that consequently, predators were critical to prevent population explosions. In the case of cougars, studies in Idaho,[27] Utah,[39] and California[44] indicate cougar populations did not significantly limit the size of the deer or elk herds. Hornocker believes the cats provide the more subtle benefits of reducing wide fluctuations in deer populations and keeping deer herds on the move by scaring and chasing them into areas that are not overbrowsed. He also believes cougars cull the sick, weak, young, old, and abnormal from the deer herd and that this reduces the possibility of disease and the passing on of less-desirable genetic characteristics to future generations.[27]

Renowned biologist Paul Errington believed that removal of some prey animals by predators increased productivity in the rest of the prey population by reducing overall competition. Thus, predation compensates for initial deaths by improving the chances of survival for other members of the herd. This concept, called *compensatory mortality*, is generally supported by research and is frequently cited in wildlife management circles as the theoretical rationale to support recreational hunting.[51] Current evidence seems to indicate that the losses of healthy or unhealthy deer to cougars are at least partly compensatory in nature.[6]

Science can only take us so far in our examination of the cougar. Objective and empirical methods have revealed much about the lions' biology, but this is only one facet of the feline enigma. A broader perspective can be gained by going back in history, to a time when the division between fact and fable was less clear. It was a time before science, when the lives of *Felis concolor* and *Homo sapiens* were more intertwined than today. It was a time when the American lion was a god.

CHAPTER 4. AN ALMOST-PERFECT PREDATOR (NOTES)

1. Kitchener, A. 1991. *The natural history of the wild cats*. Cornell University Press. Ithaca, New York.

2. Sunquist, F.C. 1987. The nature of cats. Pages 19–29 *in Kingdom of Cats*. National Wildlife Federation. Washington D.C.

3. Kiltie, R.A. 1991. How cats work. Pages 54–67 *in* J. Seidensticker and S. Lumpkin, eds. *Great cats: Majestic creatures of the wild*. Rodale Press, Emmaus, Pennsylvania.

4. Walls, G.L. 1942. *The vertebrate eye*. Harper, New York. (Cited from Kitchener 1991.)

5. Ewer, R.F. 1973. *The carnivores*. Cornell University Press, New York. (Cited from Kitchener 1991.)

6. Dixon, K.R. 1982. Mountain lion. Pages 711–727 *in* J.A. Chapman and G.A. Feldhamer, eds. *Wild mammals of North America*. John Hopkins University Press. Baltimore.

7. Melcher, J. 1987. Cougars: Anatomy of a kill. Pages 7–9 *in* K. Springer, ed. *Biologue: A journal of interpretation and discovery in the life sciences*. Teton Science School, Kelly, Wyoming.

8. Anderson, A.E. 1983. *A critical review of literature on puma (Felis concolor)*. Colorado Division of Wildlife. Special Report Number 54.

9. Lindzey, F.G. 1991. Wildlife Biologist, U.S. Fish and Wildlife Service, Wyoming Cooperative Fish and Wildlife Research Unit, University of Wyoming, Laramie, Wyoming. (Personal communication)

10. Bogue, G. and M. Ferrari. 1974. The predatory "training" of captive reared pumas. Pages 36–45 *in* R.L. Eaton, ed. *The world's cats, Vol. 3(1): Contributions to status, management and conservation*. Carnivore Research Institute, University of Washington, Seattle. (Cited from Dixon 1982.)

11. Mellen, J. 1991. Cat behavior. Pages 68–75 *in* J. Seidensticker and S. Lumpkin, eds. *Great cats: Majestic creatures of the wild*. Rodale Press, Emmaus, Pennsylvania.

12. Young, S.P. and E.A. Goldman. 1946. *The puma: Mysterious American cat*. American Wildlife Institute, Washington, D.C.

13. Leyhausen, P. 1979. *Cat bahavior: the predatory and social behavior of domestic and wild cats*. Garland STPM Press, New York. Translated by B.A. Tomkin.

14. Lopez, B. 1981. The elusive mountain lion. GEO June: 98–116.

15. Quigley, H. 1990. The complete cougar. *Wildlife Conservation* March/April: 67.

16. Tinsley, J.B. 1987. *The puma: Legendary lion of the Americas*. Texas Western Press, The University of Texas at El Paso.

17. Schmidt, R. 1992. Wildlife Technician. Associated Resource Consultants Ltd., Calgary, Alberta. (Personal communication)

18. Currier, M.J.P. 1983. *Felis concolor*. Mammalian Species No. 200, pp. 1–7. American Society of Mammalogists.

19. Halfpenny, J. and E. Biesiot. 1986. *A field guide to mammal tracking in North America*. Johnson Books, Boulder, Colorado.

20. Morse, S.C. 1991. Forest Ecologist and Wildlife Habitat Consultant. Morse and Morse Forestry. Jericho, Vermont. (Personal communication)

21. Hornocker, M.G. C. Jonkel, and L.D. Mech. 1979. Family felidae. Mountain lion (*Felis concolor*). *Wild animals of North America*. National Geographic, Washington, D.C.

22. Bowns, J.E. 1985. Predation-depredation. Pages 204–215 *in* J. Roberson and F.G. Lindzey, eds. *Proceedings of the second mountain lion workshop*, Salt Lake City, Utah.

23. Turbak, G. and A. Carey. 1986. *America's great cats*. Northland Publishing, Flagstaff, Arizona.

24. Hornocker, M.G. 1969b Stalking the mountain lion—to save him. *National Geographic* November: 638–655.

25. Lindzey, F. 1987. Mountain lion. Pages 656–668 *in* M. Novak, J.A. Baker, M.E. Obbard, and B. Malloch, eds. *Wild furbearer management and conservation in North America*. Ministry of Natural Resources, Ontario, Canada.

26. Maehr, D.S., R.C. Belden, E.D. Land, and L. Wilkins. 1990d. Food habits of panthers in southwest Florida. *Journal of Wildlife Management,* 54(3):420–423.

27. Hornocker, M.G. 1970. An analysis of mountain lion predation upon mule deer and elk in the Idaho Primitive Area. *Wildlife Monographs*, 21:1–39.

28. Ashman, D., G.C. Christensen, M.L. Hess, G.K. Tsukamoto, and M.S. Wickersham. 1983. *The mountain lion in Nevada*. Nevada Department of Wildlife, Reno.

29. Pall, O., M. Jalkotzy, and I. Ross. 1988. *The cougar in Alberta*. Fish and Wildlife Division. Alberta Forestry, Lands and Wildlife. Associated Resource Consultants. Calgary, Alberta.

30. Spalding, D.J., and J. Lesowski. 1971. Winter food of the cougar in south-central British Columbia. *Journal of Wildlife Management,* 35:378–381.

31. Seidensticker, J.C., IV, M.G. Hornocker, W.V. Wiles, and J.P. Messick. 1973. Mountain lion social organization in the Idaho Primitive Area. *Wildlife Monographs*, 35.

32. Koehler, G.M. and M.G. Hornocker. 1985. Mountain lions as a mortality factor in bobcats. Pages 170–171 *in* J. Roberson and F. Lindzey, eds. *Proceedings of the second mountain lion workshop*, Salt Lake City.

33. Yanez, J.L, J.C. Cardenas, P. Gezelle, and F.M. Jaksic. 1986. Food habits of the southernmost mountain lions (*Felis concolor*) in South America: Natural versus livestocked ranges. *Journal of Mammology*, 67(3):604–606.

34. Seidensticker, J.C. 1991a. Pumas. Pages 130–138 *in* J. Seidensticker and S. Lumpkin, eds. *Great cats: Majestic creatures of the wild*. Rodale Press. Emmaus, Pennsylvania.

35. Leopold, B.D., and P.R. Krausman. 1986. Diets of 3 predators in Big Bend National Park, Texas. *Journal of Wildlife Management*, 50(2):290–295

36. Ackerman, B.B., F.G. Lindzey, and T.P. Hemker. 1984. Cougar food habits in southern Utah. *Journal of Wildlife Management,* 48:147–155.

37. Ackerman, B.B. 1982. Cougar predation and ecological energetics in southern Utah. M.S. thesis, Utah State University, Logan.

38. Shaw, H. 1989. *Soul among lions*. Johnson Books. Boulder, Colorado.

39. Lindzey, F.G., B.B. Ackerman, D. Barnhurst, T. Becker, T.P. Hemker, S.P. Laing, C. Mecham, and W.D. Van Sickle. 1989. *Boulder-Escalante cougar project final report*. Utah Division of Wildlife Resources, Salt Lake City, Utah.

40. Danvir, R.E and F.G. Lindzey. 1981. Feeding behavior of a captive cougar on mule deer. *Encyclia*. Utah Academy of Sciences. 58:50–56.

41. Roelke, M.E. 1991. Veterinarian, Florida Panther Recovery Project, Florida Game and Fresh Water Fish Commission, Gainesville, Florida. (Personal communication)

42. Houston, A., C. Clark, J. McNamara, and M. Mangel. 1988. Dynamic models in behavioral and evolutionary ecology. *Nature*, 332:29–34. (Cited from Kitchener 1991.)

43. Logan, K.A. 1991. Wildlife Research Institute, Inc., Moscow, Idaho. (Personal communication)

44. Hopkins, R.A. 1989. Ecology of the puma in the Diablo Range, California. Ph.D. dissertation, University of California at Berkeley.

45. Cunningham, E.B. 1971. A cougar kills an elk. *Canadian Field Naturalist*. 85:253–254. (Cited from Dixon 1982.)

46. Whitfield, P. 1978. *The hunters*. Simon and Schuster, New York.

47. Dixon, K.R. 1967. *Mountain lion predation on big game and livestock in Colorado*. Job Completion Rep. Proj. W-38-R-21, Colorado Game, Fish, Parks Dept., Fort Collins, Colo. (Cited from Dixon 1982.)

48. Ashman, D. 1977. *Mountain lion investigations*. Job Performance Report, Project W-48-8. Nevada Dept. Wildl., Reno, Nevada. (Cited from Dixon 1982.)

49. de Treville, S. 1991. Wildlife Biologist. de Treville Environmental Engineering. San Diego, California. (Personal communication)

50. Hopkins, R.A. 1991. Wildlife Biologist, H.T. Harvey and Associates, Alviso, California. (Personal communication)

51. Errington, P.L. 1967. *Of predation and life*. Iowa State University Press, Ames.

COUGARS AND HUMANS

EARLY PERSPECTIVES

Cougars tread a path that winds through the mythic and earthly worlds of Native American cultures throughout the Western Hemisphere. In the mythic world, the puma was the protector of the cosmos.[1] The Zuñi of New Mexico said that the ancient ones wanted the world to be guarded by those keen of sight and scent,[2] and the puma was the sentinel of the north.[3,4,5] The Miwoks of California described the cougar as the ideal hunter, strong and brave, chief among the animals.[6] The Apaches and Hualapais of Arizona regarded the cat's wailing as an omen of death.[7] In one Navajo legend, the hero is critically wounded when witch objects are shot into his body. It is the puma who extracts these missiles of death, saving the hero's life. The Navajo also believed the puma benefited them by leaving the greater portion of their kills for the people to eat.[8] However, not everyone viewed the cougar with reverence—the Papago envisioned the lion as a flesh-eating monster.[9]

In the earthly world, many cultures believed they could imbue themselves with the puma's hunting prowess through the use of societies or fetishes. A society is a group within a tribe, usually of men, bearing a particular animal as their totem and source or power.[1] The Caiyek (Cougar Society) of Zia Pueblo in New Mexico existed to assist hunters in the chase. Members of the Caiyek believed that a supernatural ability such as successful hunting, was given to each species of animal by the Powers.[10] At Jemez Pueblo, the Cougar Society provided deer and rabbit.[11] The cougar's skill as a hunter could also be extended to warfare.[1] Membership in the Opi, a prestigious warrior society of Cochiti Pueblo, could only be obtained by killing an enemy in battle or by killing the great hunter—the puma.[10]

In some cultures, fetishes are important in transferring supernatural powers to humans. A fetish is a material object, such as a small carving, believed to contain or manifest a specific power or powers. The Hopi and Zuñi believed that fetishes were once actual beings and Zuñi hunters carried a small stone-carved mountain lion when they went deer hunting. The figure was fed every day, and upon the hunter's return, blood of the quarry was smeared on the muzzle of the fetish. At San Felipe Pueblo, mountain lion fetishes were used before a buffalo or deer hunt.[1]

The cougar was also believed to possess great magical and medicinal power. Aztec physicians prescribed pricking the breast of sick tribesmen with the sharpened bone of a puma to ward off death. Some tribes drove away illness by dangling dried cougar paws over a sick individual's head. Cougar gall was administered in extreme illness to increase the power of the ailing person to resist the disease, and ultimately to instill the cat's ferocious fighting spirit.[7] Certain warriors tied lion paws and muzzle hair to their bandoleers before going into war,[11] and the Zia Cougar Society used leggings and effigies made of puma hide in certain rites.[12]

The pervasive influence of the cougar can also be found in Native American art and architecture. The ancient Peruvian city of Cuzco was laid out in the outline of a puma and skilled artisans fashioned golden puma figurines.[13] A six-inch wooden statuette, unearthed on Marco Island, Florida, in 1895, bore the distinctive form of a living panther, and was believed to date between A.D. 1400 and A.D. 1500, when the area was occupied by the Calusa.[14]

In contrast to the reverence shown by many early cultures, Inca rulers and their subjects hunted the puma as game at the height of their civilization in ancient Peru.[7] Even so, the cat was rarely hunted for its meat. Stalking and killing a cougar, using only a spear or bow and arrow, required beating the master hunter at its own game. Few hunters possessed such skill—bear and deer no doubt proved far easier quarry.[1]

The impact of early cultures on mountain lion populations was probably minor, even though some tribes regularly killed pumas in order to gain entrance to a warrior society or to obtain materials for ceremonial or magical use. Acuff gives three reasons for this: "One, the animal was difficult to hunt. Two, the puma was revered, and one does not kill a sacred animal wantonly. [Three], human population densities were low enough that such hunting had minimal impact."[1]

To native people whose survival depended on consistently procuring adequate food, the ability of the lion to kill game with apparent ease was enormously respected, and subsequent deification of the puma is not surprising.[1] The big cat enjoyed the awe and respect of native people who shared the forests, mountains, and deserts. But in the 14th century, when the first Europeans reached the Americas, their perspective of the cougar was to be quite different.

Early explorers and settlers were driven by a desire for wealth, glory, adventure, and a tremendous religious fervor. Many of these people came from countries that were heavily settled and relatively predator-free. The Christian obsession with morality greatly influenced the European's view of native cultures and the wilderness that greeted their arrival. They saw it as their moral duty to civilize not only the "savages" but the land itself. There was no place for predators in such a world.

The cougar was not only immoral, but a competitor that vied for the abundant game of the New World and a threat to domestic livestock. As early as the 1500s, Jesuit priests in southern California were offering natives one bull for every cougar killed. In 1684, Connecticut offered a bounty of twenty shillings apiece for the killing of catamounts, the local name for the cougar. Massachusetts was paying bounties on cougars in 1742.[14] Where Native Americans offered the big cat respect, the new European immigrants felt only fear and loathing. By imposing human ethics upon wild predators it was easy to make the step from viewing them as competitors to viewing them as enemies.[15] Such simplistic thinking separated animals into two categories: beneficial (edible wild game and livestock) and injurious (all other mammals and birds).

Some native individuals did not completely acquiesce to this new vision of the sacred cougar. The Indians of peninsular California refused to kill or disturb the puma, even at the insistence of the Jesuit priests; it seems the uneaten portion of the cat's kill had long been an important source of food for these people.[7] In the early 1900s, western author Zane Grey wrote of an incident in Arizona in which where a Navajo guide refused to participate in a mountain lion hunt because that would have been tantamount to hunting a deity.[16]

From 1500 to 1900, little factual information was accumulated about the cougar. In this vacuum, the outrageous was accepted as true. Hunters and authors spun tales of a supernatural creature, more terrifying than in any of the Indian myths. Recurring themes of cowardice, gluttony, brutishness, sneakiness, and wantonness dominate. White hunters projected themselves as courageous heros destroying an evil creature that embodied traits that were considered human vices. The white man created his own mythic world—one in which the cougar was assigned malevolent attributes in order to justify his real-world extermination.[1]

As colonization spread west, the great hardwood forests of the Northeast were cleared and subdivided, effectively destroying the cougar's habitat. Alexander Crowell killed the last panther in Vermont in 1881,[17] and the last panther in Pennsylvania was shot in 1891.[18] By 1900 the cougar was effectively exterminated east of the Mississippi. As domestic cattle and sheep were released across the open plains of the West many of the native bison, pronghorn, elk, deer, and bighorn sheep were displaced.[15] Because cougars found livestock increasingly available and easy to kill, it took an occasional sheep, goat, or cow. Such *depredation*, consistently exaggerated by stockmen, did little to enhance the cougar's public image. Prevailing opinion at the turn of the century was best summed up by Theodore Roosevelt when he described the cougar during a hunt as "...the big horse-killing cat, the destroyer of the deer, the lord of stealthy murder, facing his doom with a heart both craven and cruel..."[19] Stockmen agreed, and declared war.

PREDATOR CONTROL

In early 1990, several major national magazines and newspapers carried the grisly photograph of 11 severed mountain lion heads stacked under a tree. The photograph was taken anonymously by an angry Arizona state wildlife employee. The heads represented only one-fourth of the 44 lions killed in Arizona in 1989 by professional hunters working for the U.S. Department of Agriculture's notorious Animal Damage Control (ADC) program.[20]

The U.S. Government entered the business of exterminating wild animals (many of them on public lands) in 1915, when western stockmen pressured Congress to appropriate $125,000 to wipe out wolves and coyotes and supposedly save beef for our allies in World War I.[21,22] The U.S. Biological Survey, the predecessor of the U.S. Fish and Wildlife Service, was charged with the responsibility of hiring hunters and trappers to do the job. But it was the passage of the Animal Damage Control Act of 1931 that gave birth to ADC and provided the money and authority to expand "the destruction of mountain lions, wolves, coyotes, bobcats, prairie dogs, gophers, ground squirrels, jackrabbits, and other animals injurious to agriculture, horticulture, forestry, husbandry, game, or domestic animals, or that carried disease."[21]

Between 1937 and 1970, federal employees of Animal Damage Control (ADC), derisively branded "All Dead Critters" by some of their critics, killed 7,255 cougars; 23,830 bears; 477,104 bobcats; 50,283 red wolves; 1,744 lobo wolves; 2,823,000 coyotes; and millions of other animals. After 1970, control was focused primarily on cougars, coyotes, and bobcats, because the grizzly bear and wolves were placed on the endangered species list.[23]

Federal predator control efforts are augmented by state hunters and bounty programs. Arizona originally considered the cougar an undesirable predator, and 2,400 were killed between 1918 and 1947. Efforts to eliminate the cat were accelerated in 1947 when the state began to offer a bounty varying from $50 to $100 per lion; between 1947 and 1969, over 5,400 cougars were slaughtered in Arizona.[24] Federal, state, and private hunters killed 1,775 pumas in Colorado between 1916 and 1965.[25] California paid out bounties on 12,452 cougars killed between 1907 and 1963, when the program was eliminated by the state legislature.

A good portion of this grisly total was due to the efforts of Jay Bruce, California's official lion-hunter from 1914 to 1942,[1] credited with killing almost 700 cats.[18] British Columbia lays claim to the greatest carnage, with 16,633 cats slaughtered between 1910 and 1955.[26] The bounty on cougar in British Columbia continued from 1910 to 1957; during that time the total kill probably exceeded 20,000 animals.[27] According to statistics compiled by Ronald Nowak of the U.S. Fish and Wildlife Service, a minimum of 66,665 cougars were killed within states and provinces between 1907 and 1978 .[26]

The most common methods used to control cougars were poison, trapping, and hunting with dogs.[28] At the turn of the century, predator control consisted of guarding livestock using people or dogs, as well as leghold traps, snares, and guns. Poisons were not introduced into wide use until the 1930s. The predator control arsenal contained such deadly elements as thallium sulfate, strychnine, and cyanide. The notorious poison, sodium monoflouracetate, commonly known as Compound 1080, appeared in the late 1940s. It was injected into bait carcasses, which were then transported to bait stations by vehicle or dropped from the air. Poisoned bait stations killed coyotes, bears, and eagles by the thousands. In 1972, President Nixon issued an executive order banning the use of poisons to kill predators on public lands, and the Environmental Protection Agency (EPA) disallowed the registration of such toxicants. Presidents Ford and Carter agreed with the ban, but President Reagan subsequently rescinded the original executive order, and EPA once again began registering 1080 for use in the early 1980s.[23] Today, 1080 toxic collars, which are fastened around the necks of sheep, are used to prevent attacks in Texas, Montana, Wyoming, New Mexico, and Idaho. ADC also uses strychnine for underground rodent control.[29]

Due to the cougar's low density and preference for killing its own prey, poisons were generally ineffective in eradicating it. Poisoning of lion-killed carcasses proved the most effective technique, though the kills are difficult to find. Young transient cats are probably most susceptible to poisons because of their tendency to eat unusual prey or foods.[28]

Steel-jawed, leghold traps and snares are still used today in cougar control programs though, like poisons, they are of limited effect. The cats do not respond well to scented

APPROXIMATE NUMBER OF COUGARS KILLED WITHIN STATES AND PROVINCES, 1907-1978

STATE OR PROVINCE	PERIOD	MINIMUM KILLED
Alberta	1942-1964	885
Arizona	1917-1973	8,557
British Columbia	1910-1955	16,633
California	1907-1973	12,705
Colorado	1917-1974	2,007
Idaho	1928-1973	2,781
Montana	1921-1974	503
Nevada	1917-1973	2,198
New Mexico	1917-1973	1,283
Oregon	1918-1973	6,831
Texas	1925-1973	776
Utah	1913-1978	6,253
Washington	1936-1973	5,253
	Total	66,665

Source: Nowak 1976

bait traps, so hunters use what are called blind sets: un-scented and camouflaged traps set in canyon bottoms and along rims in areas cougars are known to travel. Foothold snares can also be baited or unbaited. Some trappers even use catnip with some success. The traps or snares are then checked on a regular basis and, if a cat is found in one, it is shot. The biggest limitations to traps and snares are the time, expense, and labor necessary to make and maintain adequate sets.[28] Both poisoning and trap-ping are nonselective: many ani-mals not specifically targeted by control efforts—such as hawks, eagles, badgers, foxes, deer, javeli-na, livestock, and domestic dogs—have died in traps and snares set for other predators.

Today, hunting cougars with dogs is the most frequently used capture method, both by predator control agents and sport hunters. In 1988, the majority of cougars killed by ADC agents in Califor-nia, Nevada, Oregon, and Utah were tracked down with hunting dogs.[30] Specially trained hounds are used to track, then chase the big cats. Though a dog is no match for a cougar in speed or combat, the cats seem to consistently retreat from barking dogs. If tracking conditions are good, such as after a light snowfall, and the dogs pick up a fresh scent, the cat is no match for the hounds' endurance and will quickly seek refuge in a tree. While in the false safety of the tree, the cougar is then shot.

Until 1986, ADC was a branch of the U.S. Fish and

COUGARS KILLED BY ANIMAL DAMAGE CONTROL (ADC[A]), FY 1988[B]

Arizona	14
California	41
Colorado	13
Idaho	4
Montana	3
New Mexico	41
Oregon	14
Texas	40
Utah	28
Washington	1
Total	207

[A] Animal Damage Control is a branch of the U.S. Department of Agricluture responsible for killing predators that cause damage to livestock.

[B] Includes target (intended) and nontarget (unintended) cougars. Nontarget cougars are those killed in traps or snares set for other animals. These totals do not include additional cougars killed by state or local animal control officials.

Source: Animal Damage Control Program/Draft Environmental Impact Statement 1990.

Wildlife Service. Following the recommendation of a 1970 presidential commission that "the predator policies should be eliminated or reduced on public lands,"[21] and, due to a growing conservation ethic during the 1970s and 1980s, the role of the ADC was greatly reduced. Finally, western members of Congress, under the prodding of disgruntled stockmen, succeeded in getting ADC transferred to the U.S. De-partment of Agriculture and the program rebounded. The toll in 1989 included 237 cougars, 236 black bears, 80 gray wolves, 1,220 bobcats, 7,158 foxes, and 86,502 coyotes, 10,000 more than in 1988.[22]

Too frequently, the fiscal logic of ADC defies reason, and the ADC program is being increasingly criticized because of its enormous expense and lack of effectiveness. As Harley Shaw states, "…infor-mation available on lion popula-tion biology suggests strongly that control of lions is unlikely to occur and [is] definitely not cost efficient."[28] In 1990 the ADC program spent $29.4 million in federal dollars—$3.8 million more than 1989—plus about $15 mil-lion in state funds to destroy vast numbers of mammals and birds considered predators or pests. In 1988, California spent $3.2 million to kill 32,368 mammals—about $100 for each animal. The amount of damage the animals caused to live-stock, poultry, and crops was placed at $1.4 million. It cost twice as much to destroy the predators (41 cougars among them) than if the ranchers and farmers had been compen-sated for their losses.[20]

DEPREDATION

The killing of livestock (depredation) still fuels the political fires that advocate the killing of cougars through predator-control programs and hunting. Stockmen, biologists, and conservationists consistently cross swords over one question: How much impact do cougars have on livestock operations?

The majority of depredation permits issued to kill mountain lions are for attacks on sheep and cattle. Taking California as an example, the National Agricultural Statistics Service reports that in 1988 there were 4,600,000 cattle and calves (beef and dairy) in California and 800,000 sheep (sheep and lambs). During the same year the California Department of Fish and Game issued only 102 depredation permits for attacks on cattle, calves, sheep, and lambs.[31] In other states the situation is similar. Wain Evans states that, "Verified depredations affect less than 1 percent of New Mexico ranchers each year."[32] Suminski reports that in Nevada, the estimated annual losses of sheep to cougars averaged 0.29 percent.[33] Balancing these numbers, Fred Lindzey emphasizes that although depredation is a small problem industry-wide, local ranchers can be significantly affected.[34]

Depredation statistics indicate that cougars cause fewer livestock deaths than do other species, such as domestic dogs. Between June 1986 and June 1987, ADC information for 41 California counties showed that cougars were responsible for 5 percent of all sheep and lambs lost to predators, while domestic dogs caused 11 percent of sheep deaths and coyotes 78 percent of deaths.[35] In southwestern Utah, coyotes caused 92 percent of sheep losses and cougars were responsible for 7 percent.[36]

It was commonly assumed that most depredating lions were transients recently on their own or old lions displaced from their home range or in poor physical condition. New evidence suggests that while transient lions are more likely to kill unusual prey, healthy adult lions do kill livestock.

Hopkins found this to be the case in the Diablo Mountains of California[37] and, according to a questionnaire submitted to participants in the Second Mountain Lion Workshop, adult male and female cougars were implicated in most depredation incidents.[36]

While to humans, cattle are inappropriate prey for a mountain lion, to the opportunistic hunter, killing available and vulnerable prey, whether deer or cattle, is how the cat stays alive. In that context killing livestock is perfectly "normal" cougar behavior. Cougars will kill most species of domestic livestock, though cattle and sheep are common prey. Arizona and New Mexico suffer the most frequent losses of cattle, with incidences generally decreasing northward through the cat's range. This pattern may be largely due to ranching practices, with cattle and calf losses greatest in areas where they are born in cougar habitat.[38] However, Susan de Treville points out that cattle and lions were plentiful throughout her study area in the Big Sur region of California, yet there was little depredation, except for a few goats killed by an elderly male lion.[39] Lindzey also emphasizes that no one has demonstrated a relationship between lion density and depredation.[34] Sheep losses occur anywhere they are grazed in cougar habitat, but are greatest in the summer when the sheep are dispersed on open range. During the winter, sheep are moved to lower ground and often to fenced-in pastures.[40,41] Hopkins points out that if mountain lions were completely neutral in the prey they select, livestock would be killed in proportion to how frequently they occur in the cat's home range. Evidence shows that cattle and sheep are infrequent prey, indicating lions generally avoid them.[42]

Most cattle killed by cougars are calves less than one year old and weigh less than 200 pounds. Though they have been known to kill cows up to 800 pounds, experts feel kills in excess of 300–400 pounds are unusual.[41]

Sheep of all age classes are killed by cougars, although lambs seem to be taken more often if they are present.[36]

Cougars will kill more than one sheep in a single incident, though it will only feed on one or two. A lion in Nevada once killed 59 sheep (mostly lambs) in one attack.[33] Such occurrences of surplus killing are easily interpreted as evidence that the cougar is a "bloodthirsty" predator that "enjoys" killing. This may be true: to "enjoy" killing is probably necessary to survive. But like so much of the cat's behavior, it is not likely to be that simple.

Why does surplus killing occur? It is partly because the drive to kill an animal outweighs the need to eat it,[43] and because domestic livestock cannot or will not escape. Experiments have shown that both hungry and satiated felines continued to kill prey as long as it was presented rather than eat those already killed.[43] To a cougar, multiple kills are an efficient way to procure a lot of food in a short period of time, and are wasteful only in an artificial captive situation where 'prey' animals are kept at very high densities and are unable to escape.[44] Guggisberg explains that "the cat's urge to pounce upon a victim is constantly being reactivated by the penned-in animals helplessly milling around it. The situation it finds itself in is quite abnormal, and so, of course, is the puma's reaction. It would never be able to perform a massacre of this kind among the wild animals which form its natural prey, for they take flight the moment one of a herd has been struck down."[45]

Traditionally, there have been two approaches to cougar depredation: kill the problem lion or reduce the lion population in areas where attacks occur.[41] Most states (including California) and provinces have laws that enable livestock owners to protect their animals. Depredating lions can be destroyed if caught in the act of attacking livestock, or they can be captured and killed if the depredation incident can be verified.

Cougar population reduction is usually attempted through sport hunting—hunters are directed to specific areas experiencing livestock losses. Such general population reductions are usually ineffective. Harley Shaw advises that "in good lion habitat, attempts to control lions at any feasible level will probably accomplish nothing."[28] The complete elimination of cougars from problem regions or zones has been tried three times in New Mexico—twice to protect domestic sheep and once to protect wild sheep. None of these removals resulted in a reduction of depredation.[32] In areas where grazing is seasonal, sport hunters generally remove cougars in the winter, but livestock are not moved to these areas until summer. This provides ample time for new transient cougars to move into the area and take up residence in the hunter-created vacuum, resulting in a cougar population equal to or greater than the original population.[41] If killing resident cougars in a population results in an increase of transients, and transients are more prone to take unusual prey than resident cats, it is likely that aggressively hunting the cats could actually *increase* depredation.

Nonlethal predator control methods are available that reduce depredation. One of the most effective ways is to change livestock management practices. Economic conditions have led some ranchers to shift from sheep operations to cattle operations. In areas experiencing heavy losses to cougars, cattle ranchers have changed from cow-calf to steer operations.[36] Lindzey advises, "Pasturing livestock, primarily sheep, in more open areas and avoiding timbered areas particularly those in steep, broken terrain should reduce livestock losses to cougars."[46] For small farms raising sheep and goats, electric fences have proven effective against predators, including coyotes.[47,48] Keeping sheep more tightly herded reduces predation, but it also increases range deterioration.[36] Some sheep operations have experimented with guard dogs; these breeds are different from herding dogs and include large types such as Great Pyrenees and the Hungarian Komondor. Dogs raised with sheep and properly trained offer continual livestock protection that adapts to changes in predator behavior.[48,49] However, guard dogs have proven less effective where sheep herds are scattered thinly over the range.[36]

Two states, Colorado and Wyoming, pay ranchers compensation for cougar depredation. The lion was classified as a game animal in Colorado in 1965 and the Division of Wildlife (DOW) became liable for damages at that time. Although the original legislation was contested, it was upheld by the courts;[36] Colorado paid $44,959 in compensation for livestock losses between 1990 and 1991, according to Cathy Moser of the DOW's Terrestrial Section.

John Talbott, Assistant Chief Game Warden for the Wyoming Game and Fish Department (WGFD), explains that his department is responsible for damage to domestic livestock by trophy game animals, and that the cougar became a game animal in 1981. Most of Wyoming's losses are sheep rather than cattle, and not surprisingly, the biggest point of contention between state wildlife officials and ranchers is the magnitude of such losses. WGFD rarely pays for the entire loss. No compensation is allowed in either state if a landowner does not permit hunting on his property.

Talbott believes Wyoming's compensation program "increases tolerance of the cougars and helps ranchers view them as a bona fide wildlife resource that people like to see out there." Both he and Moser think the programs increase cooperation between property owners and the states. Talbott further points out that the expense of compensation programs is not just in the money paid to ranchers. There are also the substantial costs of monitoring both sheep and lions, verifying losses, negotiating compensation, and administrative time. On the negative side of the issue is the question of whether a public agency managing a public resource, frequently on public land, should be reimbursing ranchers for losses of private property.

HUNTING

The 1960s brought a new perspective on predators and a limited degree of protection for the cougar as state legislatures and wildlife managers in most of the western states shifted the big cat's official status from injurious predator to game animal. Nevada reclassified the cougar as a game animal in 1965; Washington did so in 1966, followed by Utah in 1967 and California in 1969. All other western states followed suit. Two Canadian provinces, Alberta and British Columbia, did likewise. California set a new precedent in 1990 when residents passed a referendum giving the cougar complete protection from sport hunting. At the other extreme is Texas, where the lion is still considered a varmint and receives no protection from the state whatsoever.[50]

Hunting seasons vary in length from year-round to one month, with bag limits usually 1 cougar per season per person. Most states require a permit. Northern states usually set their seasons in late fall and winter, when snow provides the best conditions for tracking with dogs. Some states time their hunting seasons so they do not conflict with other big-game seasons and to reduce conflicts between cougar hunters and their dogs and people hunting deer and elk. Other states time seasons to avoid cougar birth peaks. This is thought to provide a measure of protection for small, vulnerable kittens and presumably reduces the number of young kittens orphaned when their mothers are killed (more on this later). Texas and Oregon also allow trapping as a method of sport harvest.[41]

A number of states offer special "pursuit-only" seasons. During pursuit-only seasons, hunters are allowed to chase and tree cats, but not to kill them. This provides a way for hunters to train and condition their dogs and is also used by wildlife photographers to get a picture of this elusive animal in the wild; however, some experts point out that cougars can still be injured or killed during such seasons. Lindzey explains: "Permanent physical damage to a mountain lion may result from prolonged or frequent chases. Also, small kittens are as vulnerable to being killed by dogs during these seasons as they are during regular sport-hunting seasons."[41]

Successful cougar hunting requires the use of specially trained tracking hounds and sometimes involves several days spent trailing the elusive cats through miles of rugged terrain. Since few hunters are willing to make such an investment in time or effort to train dogs, they usually employ the services of a hunting guide. For a fee of $1,500 to $5,000, the guide supplies the food, lodging, hounds, horses, four-wheel-drive truck, and familiarity with the local terrain. Some hunting guides use CB radios, walkie-

talkies, and fit their hounds with special radio collars, which allow the guide and hunter to radio track the hounds while the hounds trail the cougar. The radio collars frequently contain a switch that is triggered when the dog tips its head back for an extended period, indicating that a cougar has been treed.

While most hunting guides run legitimate operations, the expense of long pursuits and the impatience of clients to bag a trophy cat entice some guides to provide a higher level of convenience in the form of "will-call" (as in, "When we have your cougar treed, we will call you") or "shootout" (as in, "All you have to do is shoot it out of the tree") hunts.[50] The guide puts a list of clients in his pocket, then heads out into the woods to find and track a cougar. Once he has a cat treed he radios the client or leaves the cat under the watchful eye of a helper and drives to the nearest telephone. The client then flies and drives to the location of the treed cougar to collect his trophy. As a result, cougars remain up in the tree for days at a time, under a death watch. If it jumps from the tree it is simply treed again, until the client arrives. (Bears are also frequent victims of will-call hunts.) Although keeping a cougar in a tree overnight does violate some state laws that prohibit hunting at night, this form of hunting is not illegal. Many question the morality of these will-call hunts, though. Bill Powers, coordinator of Arizona's Operation Game Thief silent-witness program, says "I'd guess that around 30 percent of the guided hunts in Arizona are will-call hunts, and that's probably conservative."[50]

Cougar hunting is growing in popularity. In those states that allow lion hunting, the number of permits has risen steadily over the last decade. Permit sales have more than doubled in Utah during the past ten years, with little or no increase in the number of lions killed.[46] Utah charges state residents only $12 for a license, plus a $27 lion permit fee. Nonresidents must pay $40 for the license, and $252 for a lion permit. A mountain lion hunting license in Colorado costs $30 for a resident and $250 for a nonresident. Revenues from license and tag sales rarely cover the costs of cougar research and management programs. Most of the money to be made from cougar hunting goes to guides, with local economies probably receiving a portion of the revenue.[41]

With so much time, energy, and money expended on cougar hunting, one question eventually presents itself: What impact does hunting have on mountain lion populations? It's a simple enough question, but asking it sparks immediate debate between hunters, antihunters, and nonhunters. Unfortunately, such debates generate more heat than light, and when these factions turn to wildlife biologists, no simple answers are available. Surprisingly little effort has been devoted to gaining an understanding of how sport hunting affects cougar populations.[46]

Many hunters, wildlife managers, and biologists insist the hunting of cougars is necessary to keep cougar populations healthy, prevent overpopulation, and protect deer herds. None of these arguments is based on sound biology. The primary justification of recreational hunting in contemporary society is based on the notion that wildlife populations produce a "harvestable surplus" of individuals,[51] and that removal of this surplus benefits the population as a whole by reducing competition. For example, by killing a portion of a mule deer herd there

is less competition for forage within the remaining herd, resulting in less starvation. Thus, the initial deaths due to hunting "compensate for," or reduce other forms of natural mortality such as starvation. Biologists such as Paul Errington believe each species population has surplus individuals whose death is assured, regardless of the literal cause of death. Whether the surplus individuals die by starvation, predation, or hunting makes no difference, and advocates of this compensatory-mortality theory view hunting as a substitute form of predation.[52]

While most recreational hunting programs are based on this theory of "harvesting the surplus," and a significant body of research supports it, many of the studies were conducted on species such as deer, muskrats, and quail, animals that exist in large numbers and exhibit large population fluctuations. It may be more difficult to apply such reasoning to pumas, low-density predators whose populations appear to fluctuate very little and whose population dynamics are poorly understood.

Hunting cougars probably never completely compensates for natural mortality, and in some cases may even add to it. Lindzey and his colleagues found this to be the case while studying survival rates of mountain lions in southern Utah. "Hunting mortality will *not be fully compensated for* [emphasis added] by a reduction in other sources of

---

COUGAR SPORT KILL, 1987-1990

	1987	1988	1989	1990
Arizona	236	206	186	225
British Columbia	144	194	212	254
Colorado	180	178	183	227
Idaho [1]	300	350	340	350
Nevada	82	118	152	52
New Mexico	101	104	108	112
Oregon	166	132	145	155
Texas	131	170	160	150
Utah	131	162	160	217
Washington	60	89	85	97
Wyoming	102	84	60	62
	1986/87	1987/88	1988/89	1989/90
Alberta	33	33	34	47
Montana	171	158	166	228

[1] Includes cougars killed for attacking livestock.
Sources: Arizona Game and Fish Department; Colorado Division of Wildlife, Idaho Department of Fish and Game; Montana Department of Fish, Wildlife and Parks; Nevada Department of Wildlife, New Mexico Department of Game and Fish; Oregon Department of Fish and Wildlife; Texas Parks and Wildlife Department; Utah Division of Wildlife Resources, Washington Department of Wildlife; and Wyoming Game and Fish Department.

mortality. Intraspecific killings [fighting] and debilitating injuries resulting from attempts to capture prey will occur even in populations where densities are reduced by hunting. The degree to which hunting is *additive* [emphasis added] to other forms of mortality needs to be identified...."[53]

Sport hunting advocates point to the evidence that cougar populations appear to tolerate tremendously high levels of hunting mortality and still recover. Kerry Murphy monitored the response of a small population of western Montana lions to heavy sport hunting. He concluded that over 50 percent of the resident adults in the area were killed, but were replaced by young adults raised in the area or transients immigrating from surrounding areas.[54] David Ashman and his coworkers in Nevada believe that even under removal of 30 to 50 percent of lion populations, the cats are capable of rapidly replacing annual losses.[55] While these examples certainly testify to the puma's resilience, they tell little about the effect of hunting on the cat's intricate population dynamics.

Another study in southern Utah indicates that, when hunting mortality is combined with high natural mortality, cougars may not be so resilient. Biologists simulated a cougar hunt by removing 27 percent of the cats from a population. Seven lions were placed in captivity or transported out of the study area the first year, while another three died of natural causes the following year. By the second year the population had failed to recover to its preremoval level. The investigators concluded that "Failure of the population to recover to preremoval level two years later and its inability to replace one of three resident adults that died the second year, suggests the population would not have recovered as quickly from a second year's harvest of similar intensity.

The effect of hunting on cougar populations will depend both on level of harvest and sex and age of cougars removed; populations will be most sensitive to loss of resident adult females."[56]

John Laundre and Donald Streubal, who are studying cougar ecology and behavior in Idaho, wonder about the effect of hunting on kitten mortality. "The fact that males kill kittens, [has been] documented in earlier studies as well as ours. According to evolutionary theory, males would not kill their own kittens," writes Streubel.[57] "Therefore, if hunting selects males from the population, new males would be more frequently moving into new home [ranges] and thus increasing chances of non-relatedness with resident kittens. This would seem to increase the mortality of kittens."

Most states prohibit killing females with kittens or spotted kittens. However, it may be difficult for hunters to

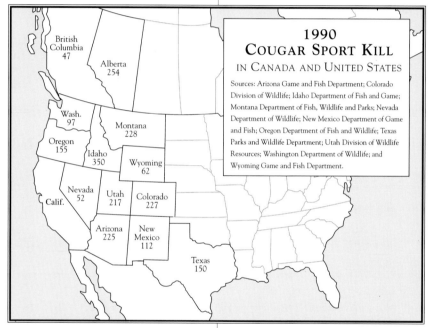

1990 COUGAR SPORT KILL
IN CANADA AND UNITED STATES

Sources: Arizona Game and Fish Department; Colorado Division of Wildlife; Idaho Department of Fish and Game; Montana Department of Fish, Wildlife and Parks; Nevada Department of Wildlife; New Mexico Department of Game and Fish; Oregon Department of Fish and Wildlife; Texas Parks and Wildlife Department; Utah Division of Wildlife Resources; Washington Department of Wildlife; and Wyoming Game and Fish Department.

British Columbia 47
Alberta 254
Wash. 97
Oregon 155
Montana 228
Idaho 350
Wyoming 62
Nevada 52
Calif.
Utah 217
Colorado 227
Arizona 225
New Mexico 112
Texas 150

differentiate females with kittens from other mountain lions because young are often not with their mothers. Biologist Dan Barnhurst observed that the tracks of newborn to 6-month-old kittens were found with their mother's only 19 percent of the time, while tracks of 7- to 12-month old kittens were found with their mother's tracks 43 percent of the time. Tracks are the sign most used by hunters, but even if a hunter wished to comply with the laws and avoid killing spotted kittens or females with kittens, 80 percent of the time he would have no way of knowing that the female has kittens.[58]

Barnhurst also examined the vulnerability of cougars to hunting. For kittens less than six months old, being orphaned is probably the main source of mortality in heavily hunted populations. A second source of hunting-related kitten mortality is that of kittens being killed by dogs. The risk of this is greatest for kittens less than three months old, because the mother must return frequently to the den to nurse them. The tracks she leaves will eventually lead dogs to the kittens. Since the kittens are too young to climb trees or outrun the dogs, they may be caught on the ground and killed before the hunter is aware of their presence.[58] This situation emphasizes why even pursuit-only seasons can result in lions being killed.

"Unfortunately, the current sport hunting season in many states begins in the fall and *it is probable that in some areas, cub mortality from maulings and orphaning is as significant as adult harvest* [emphasis added]," writes Thomas Hemker and his colleagues. "The degree that hunting and nonhunting deaths compensate for each other is not clear, although it seems that causes of natural mortality are at least partially independent of hunting. Consequently, it seems probable that cub survival would be lower in hunted populations where either sex of adult cougars may be removed."[59]

Experts hope that some better answers to these perplexing hunting questions will be provided by a 10-year research study currently underway in the San Andres Mountains of southern New Mexico. Because the mountains lie within the U.S. Army's White Sands Missile Range, cougar hunting has been prohibited. It will be the first long-term intensive study of unhunted cougars in a desert environment. Biologists Kenney Logan, Linda Sweanor, and Frank Smith of the Wildlife Research Institute in Moscow, Idaho, are manipulating the resident lion population by removing a portion of the cats to simulate an "overharvest." After studying the general ecology of the lion population for five years, they removed 70 percent of the lions (13 adults and subadults) from the southern one-third of the San Andres Range. The cats were then translocated to an area in northern New Mexico, where another biologist will monitor their activity. Logan says the project has four objectives:

1. To determine the effects of the removal on lion population dynamics. This includes the immigration of transients, emigration (dispersal) of kittens, changes in the behavior of the lions toward each other, and general distribution and movement of the lions in the study area.

2. To determine the effects of the removal on lion social organization. This includes changes in the ratio of males to females, changes in the age classes of lions (residents, transients, and kittens), or shifts in home range size and overlap.

3. To determine the effects of lion removal on the survival of desert mule deer (*Odocoileus hemionus crookeri*) and desert bighorn sheep (*Ovis canadensis mexicana*), which the lions prey on in the San Andres.

4. To monitor the behavior of the translocated mountain lions.

Scheduled for completion in 1995, the project is a cooperative effort between the New Mexico Department of Fish and Game, the U.S. Fish and Wildlife Service, and the White Sands Missile Range.[60]

Existing research provides little evidence that sport hunting benefits cougar populations by keeping them "healthy." As to whether lions overpopulate or devastate deer herds, studies indicate that the cat's social behavior generally keeps their numbers in check[28,61] and that their impact on healthy deer populations is thought to be minimal.[62] Nor does hunting mountain lions reduce incidents of depredation.[36] Mountain lion sport hunting exists today primarily to provide a recreational experience for hunters who want to bag a trophy.

One fact is certain, however: 2,176 cougars died at the hands of hunters in western North America in 1990. Idaho lead the pack with 350 lions killed, followed by Alberta with 254, and Montana at 228. Sport hunting is still the greatest known cause of death in cougars.

POACHING

On November 16, 1990, state and federal authorities converged on a ranch near Lockwood, California. What they found were the skulls, heads, and hides of mountain lions, Bengal tigers, spotted leopards, black leopards, and jaguars—remnants of illegal "hunts" conducted by the ranch owners, Floyd and Dawn Patterson.[63] "Big game hunters" paid the Pattersons up to $3,500 for the privilege of shooting the big cats and taking their stuffed carcasses home as trophies. Most of the animals were thought to have been surplus zoo animals and many were simply shot in the stock trailer they were delivered in. One cat was dragged out with a lasso around its neck and shot just out-

side the door.[64] The Pattersons were tried and convicted on 42 counts of violating state wildlife laws.[65] Federal agents are still investigating the crimes and may yet file additional charges, which carry even more severe penalties.

The effect of poaching on cougar populations in North America is unknown, but according to the U.S. Fish and Wildlife Service (FWS), trade in illegal animal parts is a $200 million a year business, and growing, a 100 percent increase since 1980. John Turner, FWS Director, says, "Our wildlife is under siege."[66] The international trade in wildlife, both legal and illegal, is a $5 billion-a-year business, and the United States is the largest consumer, accounting for $1 billion of the revenue annually.[67]

Illegally trapped cougars and endangered jaguars are purchased by unscrupulous outfitters for hunters willing to pay big trophy fees.[68] Cougars and bighorns are killed for their hides and heads. Bear gall bladders are sold as aphrodisiacs and their jaws, teeth and claws for jewelry. Elk and deer are killed and their hides, meat, and antlers sold. Major purchasers of poached goods are Asian medicine shops and markets. In the Orient, animal parts such as antlers and bear and cougar gall bladders are believed to have strong curative powers.

No longer simply an occasional deer taken out of season or a couple of fish over the limit, the age of large-scale commercial poaching has arrived. Skilled, organized, and well-equipped teams of poachers are decimating our nation's wildlife and reaping obscene profits in the process. According to Larry Farnsworth, commercial poaching is a "nationwide problem of a considerable magnitude. The data...indicates that commercial poaching is one of the most underreported crimes in the country." Farnsworth estimated the minimum value of the illegal sale of wildlife at $175,100,773 and feels this number is extremely low.[69]

National parks, once seen as refuges, are becoming the killing fields of our wildlife. Obsessed trophy hunters in search of the biggest prizes are slipping into parks to shoot mountain lions, elk, deer, grizzlies, and bighorn sheep. Their reward is an entry in a record book, wall mounts, pictures in albums, and quick profits.[68] Black bears are slaughtered by the hundreds in Great Smoky Mountains National Park; hunters in Alaska's Denali National Park use small airplanes to gun down entire packs of wolves for their valuable pelts; poachers in Rocky Mountain National Park target bighorn sheep, deer, and elk. Rangers in Alaska consider illegal trophy hunting their worst problem.[67]

Poaching is considered by some experts to be less of a threat to cougars due to the difficulty of hunting lions without dogs and the low value of the pelt; however, this may be changing. In Los Angeles, a Korean buyer placed orders for 300 bear paws, 14 bear gall bladders, and 15 cougar gall bladders.[70] The California Department of Fish and Game reports there were 43 known cougars illegally killed between 1984 and 1990. In 1988, the Washington Department of Game states that of the 121 cougars killed in the state, 32 of them were illegal.[30] With bear gall bladders going for $540 per ounce and a record-sized bighorn sheep head worth $50,000, the incentive to poach is high. It is also important to note that cougar gall bladders are visually indistinguishable from bear gall bladders.

Heavy poaching of deer herds can have indirect impacts on cougars by removing potential prey. Based on information provided by California, Oregon, Idaho, Michigan, Nevada, Texas, Washington, and Wisconsin, roughly one-half or more of some fish and game species that are taken each year might be taken illegally by poachers. California Department of Fish and Game estimates, for example, that of the approximately 160,000 deer taken in California in 1984, roughly 100,000, or 62 percent were killed illegally.[71]

Poachers face little risk of being caught. There are only 7,200 state game wardens and fewer than 200 federal wildlife agents nationwide, to enforce the myriad wildlife laws.[72] According to Pete Bontadelli, former director of

California Department of Fish and Game, "California has 330 game wardens in the field, which comes out to about 1 warden for every 300,000 acres. A past study showed we would need five times the current warden force to do the job effectively."[73] Bontadelli says their poaching apprehension rate is about 4 percent, which is higher than some states that estimate their violator apprehension rate between 1 and 2 percent. Most violations are not even reported. Canadian wildlife officials hired a man in 1987 to commit a variety of hunting violations, including poaching. Of the 762 crimes, only 8 (1.1 percent) were ever reported.[67]

Poachers also face little chance of severe punishment should they be caught. While Floyd Patterson was sentenced to six months in jail and fined $28,200 and his wife Dawn was fined $14,100 and sentenced to 200 hours of community service,[74] they were the exceptions. Most courts, straining under an overwhelming docket of crimes such as murder, rape, robbery, and drug-related crimes tend to look upon wildlife violations as minor infractions. Guilty violators usually walk away with small fines or a suspended sentence. Under such circumstances, poaching has the ominous potential to become yet another obstacle to the cougar's survival.

COUGAR ATTACKS ON HUMANS

American folklore is filled with stories of the "Devil Cat" descending from the mountains, announcing its presence with a bloodcurdling scream, and searching for any opportunity to drag helpless victims off into the night. Such stories have all the elements of good fiction. Unfortunately, the shy and secretive nature of the cougar helped to nurture these fables.

By the early 1900s a different version of the mountain lion was slowly beginning to emerge. Tracy Storer wrote in 1923 that, "It is the general belief among naturalists and well informed laymen that the…Mountain Lion…does not ordinarily attack human beings. This belief is strengthened by the experience of many thousands of people who have camped and lived in the range of the mountain lion…without being harmed in any way."[75] Early puma researcher Frank Hibben claimed, "Man, who upon greater acquaintance with the cougar loses much of his dread of the animal…[will] find a curious, gentle, and very likeable disposition supplanting the vicious side."[76] Even Teddy Roosevelt changed his view, claiming "that it would be no more dangerous to sleep in woods populated with mountain lions than if they were ordinary house cats…"[77]

There is no question that cougars attack people on occasion. The earliest recorded fatal attack in the United States is thought to have been a 58-year-old man living in Chester County, Pennsylvania, in 1751.[7] The most recent was an 18-year-old jogger killed near Idaho Springs, Colorado, in January 1991.[78] In order to assess the risk lions pose, other important questions must be answered: How frequently do these attacks occur? Why do they occur? What can be done to prevent future attacks?

In an attempt to get some answers, Paul Beier conducted a detailed review and analysis of cougar attacks on humans in the United States and Canada. Only those cases where a cougar bit, clawed, or knocked down a human were considered. Maulings by captive cougars and cases in which a person (e.g., a cougar hunter) deliberately approached or harassed a wild cougar were excluded. Each report was included only if it could be verified by a newspaper or other published account that included statements from medical personnel, law enforcement officers, wildlife officials, or park rangers. Applying this criteria, Beier found that from 1890 to 1990, there were 53 recorded cougar attacks in the United States and Canada. There were 9 fatal attacks resulting in 10 deaths and 44 nonfatal attacks resulting in 48 injuries. The greater number of victims is because there were 2 victims in 5 of the attacks.[79]

Children were found to be more vulnerable than adults, making up 64 percent of the victims. Those 5 to 9 years old were in the highest risk group. Whether or not the child was with an adult also seemed to influence their vulnerability. Of 37 child victims, 35 percent were alone, 43 percent were in groups of children, and 22 percent were accompanied by adults. Adults made up 36 percent of the victims, and the majority (11 of 17), were alone when attacked.[79]

Underweight yearling lions (12 to 23 months old) seem more inclined to attack people, and made up 40 percent of the offending cats. At this age an immature cougar increasingly hunts without help from its mother and by 14 to 24 months of age it moves into a new and often unfamiliar home range.[55,61] "Under these stresses, some yearlings may have difficulty capturing wild prey," writes Beier. "The low body mass of most yearling attackers suggests that this may be a factor. Two of the underweight yearling attackers also had porcupine quills in their throat." In addition, the report shows that half of attacking adult lions were noticeably underweight.

Only two offending cougars were found to have a disease or injury. One was probably rabid and caused two deaths from a single attack near Morgan Hill, California, in 1909. This is the only known case of rabies being transmitted from a cougar to humans; both victims died of the disease, not from the physical injuries.[75] The second diseased cougar had cataracts and was killed near Cowichan Lake, British Columbia, in 1916.

British Columbia accounts for over half (57 percent) of all recorded attacks, with the hot spot being Vancouver Island, a 12,408-square-mile island with 300,000 human residents. Twenty of the 53 attacks (38 percent) took place on Vancouver Island, 10 on mainland British Columbia, 5 in Texas, 4 in California, 3 each in Alberta and Colorado, 2 each in Arizona, Montana, and Washington, and 1 each in New Mexico and Nevada.[79] Experts are at a loss to explain why there is such a concen-

tration of attacks on Vancouver Island. Dennis Pemble, a British Columbia wildlife-control officer, thinks the reason is because of the island's lush and heavy cover, which allows the cats to stalk close without being detected.[80] Others have observed that smaller prey, such as porcupines, cottontail rabbits, and opossums are absent from the island. This lack of small prey may prove stressful to yearling lions less proficient at taking deer, and may contribute to attacks on humans.[79]

Across the Georgia Strait, on mainland British Columbia, Pemble is frequently called upon to kill or capture and move mountain lions that have wandered into the suburban neighborhoods of North and West Vancouver, a city of almost a half-million people. Excellent deer and cougar habitat exists only a few miles from the center of the city, and occasionally lions will take a pet dog or cat. Pemble notes that most of the cats he captures in or near Vancouver are young animals or adult males.[81] In July 1991, two children and their teacher were mauled by a lion near the town of Lillooet, about 120 miles northeast of Vancouver.[80] Seidensticker notes that what impresses him is not the number of attacks in the Vancouver area but how really *few* there have been, given the close proximity of mountain lions and people.[81]

Beier's study further points out that aggressive behavior on the part of intended victims may discourage a lion about to attack or even repel an attack in progress. This differs from the more passive practice of playing dead or curling up in a fetal position during bear attacks. Because the cougar is such a skilled stalker, few victims actually saw the cat before being clawed or bitten. In those individuals who did have time to react, shouting, swinging a stick, waving arms above the head, or throwing rocks clearly deterred the cougar from carrying out an attack. It also seems advisable not to run. In at least two cases, running appeared to stimulate the cougar to chase and attack the victim. The majority of people with whom pumas actually made physical contact

fought back with bare hands, a stick, a knife, a jacket, or a rock. These efforts usually succeeded in driving off the cat. Even children who were alone were able to repel the cougar by fighting back.[79]

In a recent issue of *Smithsonian*, Seidensticker and Lumpkin speculated as to what would motivate a cougar to attack a human. Like other big cats, mountain lions specialize in killing large mammals with hooves, primarily deer and elk. A human standing up is just not the right shape for a cat's prey. An erect person's head and neck are in the wrong place, and most adults are taller than even the largest of the cougar's prey species. The position of the neck is most important, for that is where the cat must deliver the killing bite. However, a person bending over, squatting, or running may present a more attractive prey configuration to a cougar. The authors point out that tigers sometimes kill Asian rubber tappers and grass cutters who bend over frequently while working, or people who go out at night and squat to relieve themselves. They suggest that perhaps the Colorado jogger who was recently killed had attracted the cat's attention as he ran along, then stopped and crouched down to tie a loose shoelace.[81]

Ironically, the animal that causes more human deaths than any other is not the cougar, but the cougar's primary prey: deer. According to the National Highway Safety Administration, deer were responsible for 130 human fatalities in 1989 alone; most of these were due to collisions between the animals and motor vehicles.[82] (The number of deer killed in these accidents will be discussed in the next section.) But deer are not the only deadly threats to humans. Each year in the United States, domestic dogs kill 18 to 20 people and inflict 200,000 injuries requiring stitches,[83] bee stings are fatal to over 40 individuals, and rattlesnakes inflict 5,000 bites resulting in 12 human deaths.[84] Yet none of these very real hazards seem to stir near the interest of cougar sightings. Writers Dan Bensimhom and Mary Brophy suggest that it would be wise to "forget about lions and tigers and bears. Just keep a sharp eye out for Bambi, bees, and man's best friend."[82]

Mountain lion attacks do seem to have increased in the last 20 years. There were more fatal attacks during the last 21 years (6) than during the previous 80 years (4). Authorities generally believe there are two reasons for the increase: mountain lion populations are growing in some areas because states and provinces have changed the cats' status from bountied predator to a game species and, in the case of California, have given the puma complete protection. Simultaneously, human populations are growing, along with their use of wildlands, which has increased the potential for encounters.[79]

Shaw observes that there has likely been a marked change in the way people react to seeing a cougar in the wild. Early hunters and ranchers would not have made an "official" report of a sighting, or even of a threatening incident. The lion was usually shot whether it threatened or not. Modern, unarmed hikers are more likely to report a sighting. When lions show up near more populated areas the "threat" becomes an official problem, usually with media involvement. Shaw suspects that "to some extent, we're dealing with an increase in noise, not numbers."[85]

Some people have strongly suggested that attacks can be prevented through regular hunting of cougars; however, there is no evidence that cougars are more likely to attack humans in unhunted areas.[79] As previously mentioned, 57 percent of all attacks took place in British Columbia, yet hunters and predator control agents kill almost 200 cougars in the province annually.[27] Additionally, the number of attacks in Texas (5) and in Colorado (4), both of which allow hunting, does not differ significantly from California (4), where sport hunting has been illegal since 1972.

In an effort to understand what is behind these increasing encounters between cougars and people, the first Mountain Lion-Human Interaction Symposium and

Workshop was held in Denver, Colorado, in April 1991. Hundreds of cougar researchers, wildlife managers, conservationists (including this author), and reporters from across North America gathered to hear the presentation of papers, to participate in discussions, to compare notes, and to talk. One point frequently made was about the increasing "urban/wilderness interface." Simply put, this is the growing fringe of urban areas that is pushing deeper into prime mountain lion habitat. Jim Halfpenny, a lion researcher from the University of Colorado, emphasized the need for studies on lions near urban areas. Dennis Pemble from British Columbia and several wildlife officers from Colorado Department of Wildlife spoke at length about having to increasingly respond to reported lions in suburban areas. By the end of the three-day conference it was clear that not much was known about lion behavior and encounters; however, there seemed to be agreement on one point: there is an important need to educate the public about cougars and how to live with them.

Recent events in southern California may portend what could happen if wildlife and land managers do not take an aggressive approach to educating the public about mountain lions. In 1986, two children were mauled by cougars within a few months of each other in Ronald W. Caspers Wilderness Park, east of San Juan Capistrano. The attacks were the first in California since 1909. In August 1991, the parents of the first child won a lawsuit against Orange County, which has jurisdiction over the park, and were awarded $2 million.[86] While the victim's lawyer claimed the county had been negligent in warning visitors about lions in the park, the case has ominous implications for resource agencies being held liable for the behavior of wildlife. Orange County plans to appeal the case, but the second victim is waiting in the wings with another lawsuit. Sadly, in August 1992, the Orange County Board of Supervisors banned all children under the age of 18 from Caspers Wilderness Park.[87]

HABITAT LOSS
AND FRAGMENTATION

When our ancestors first set foot in New England they beheld magnificent, primeval forests that would have rivaled today's few remaining old-growth forests in the Northwest. Huge, old trees, stately white pines 200 feet or more in height, hemlocks, maples, beeches, and birches thrived among a richly diverse community of trees and shrubs. Trees of different heights and an extraordinary mix of species created an equally varied and rich range of opportunities for birds, mammals, and all other fauna. Through this paradise trod the catamount, or eastern panther, hunting the abundant white-tailed deer.[88]

Within a mere 200 to 300 years it was all gone—the forests and the wildlife. Colonial land clearing and burning for settlements was only the beginning. By the middle of the nineteenth century, most forests had been cut over two or three times, exploited for lumber, pulp, fuel, charcoal, potash, tannin, pitch, and ship stores. Market hunting, along with ongoing, unregulated hunting and trapping, resulted in the astonishing scarcity of many game species (notably deer) by the late 1700s. All predators and any animal with a marketable hide were threatened or locally exterminated by 1900. The panther, eastern timber wolf, wolverine, pine martin, fisher, and even the beaver disappeared completely.[88]

The cougar survives in western North America primarily because of 700 million acres set aside as public land. Maurice Hornocker acknowledges the importance of this habitat and credits the Wilderness Act of 1964 as an example of legislation beneficial to cougars. While the national forests, national parks, wildlife refuges, and other state and federal lands provide a measure of protection, loss of critical habitat is still the greatest single threat to wildlife—and the cougar is no exception.

Urban, residential, and agricultural development encroaches on cougar habitat throughout North America. In Colorado, the growing urban corridor that extends along the eastern shoulder of the Rocky Mountains, from Boulder south to Denver and Colorado Springs, presses in on the margins of cougar country. Rampant growth on Florida's coasts is squeezing the Everglades on both sides and threatening the few remaining panthers. The urban sprawl of Tucson and other communities is adjacent to some of Arizona's densest cougar populations, which are located in the southeast corner of the state. Since 1945, California has lost over 5 million acres of wildlife habitat and, from 1948 to 1990, the state's human population rose from 9.6 million to 30 million. New residents have a penchant for settling in the brushy chaparral country of the western Sierra Nevada and in the coastal mountains. Both areas are prime mountain lion habitat. San Diego, Los Angeles, and the San Francisco Bay Area all have adjacent mountain lion populations.

As the stress of urban living begins to take its toll, more and more people seek to escape, finding a temporary refuge in the public lands. Many of the growing cities in the West provide easy access to nearby national parks, national forests, and other public lands, and annual visitation to America's national parks now exceeds 260 million a year. Increasing numbers of visitors backpack in the most remote wilderness areas—areas that are home to the cougar.

The U.S. Forest Service, Bureau of Land Management, and U.S. Fish and Wildlife Service administer the public lands under a policy of multiple use. This allows such activities as logging, mining, livestock grazing, and recreational uses such as hunting, off-road vehicles, and snowmobiles. Increased logging and mining operations mean more roads, which further subdivides valuable wildlife habitat. Cougar research in southern Utah and northern Arizona showed that the cats tend to avoid areas of high road densities and recent clear cuts.[89] Extensive dirt road networks in an area also make cougars more vulnerable to hunting. Dan Barnhurst believes that road closures would be very effective in limiting the number of cougars killed during a hunting season and could be used for specific goals such as discouraging hunting in a drainage known to be occupied by a female and kittens. He further states, "Since increased road access increases cougar vulnerability, the potential impact on the cougar population should be considered in the environmental impact statement of any planned projects that include construction of new roads (i.e., timber sales and fossil fuels or mineral exploration).[58]

Paved roads are probably the most efficient wildlife slaughtering mechanisms ever devised. Each year, millions of wild animals are killed on America's highways. The California Department of Transportation estimates that automobiles kill almost 20,000 mule deer each year, a number equal to deer killed by hunters annually.[90] The toll these collisions have on human life was mentioned in the previous section. When combined with development, highways pose a triple threat to wildlife: as development reduces the amount of available habitat and squeezes remaining wildlife into smaller and more isolated pockets, high-speed traffic on larger and wider highways kills more and more of the remaining population.[91] Imagine the risk a mountain lion faces in attempting to cross an eight-lane interstate freeway. Of the 32 cougars Paul Beier has collared in the Santa Ana Mountains of southern California, nine have been hit by cars. Only two survived.[92]

"In the long run, these habitat fragmenting forces may be more degrading to North America's wildlife population than actual loss of habitat acreage," says Larry Harris, a professor at the University of Florida. According to Harris, habitat fragmentation results in four major consequences for wildlife:

1. Loss of "area-sensitive" species, animals whose existence and successful reproduction depend on the size of the habitat area in which they occur. The cougar,

bobcat, and black bear fall into this category.

2. Large species that are highly mobile and occur at low densities under the best of conditions are lost. Again, the cougar is representative.

3. When coupled with the loss of large native carnivores, fragmented and human-altered landscapes (providing artificial sources of food and shelter) become dominated by exotic or already common species.

4. Inbreeding begins to occur in isolated populations of low density, such as the endangered Florida panther.[91]

The cougar is an "area-sensitive" species, requiring a home range so great as to demand large areas for sustenance. Without a sufficiently large territory it cannot find sufficient food or freely interbreed. Lack of available mates leads to inbreeding, which leads to losses of libido, fertility, and reproduction.[93]

Preservation of large tracts of natural land certainly seems to be the solution. But how big is big enough? Even our largest national parks are losing species. William Newmark of the University of Michigan has surveyed the history of local extinctions of mammals in national parks of western North America and has made a startling discovery. Since 14 western parks were established, Newmark documented 44 local extinctions among carnivores, ungulates, hares, and rabbits, the most commonly documented species. The main problem appears to be that even our largest parks are too small.[94]

Working with the isolated population of cougars in the Santa Ana Mountains, Paul Beier has estimated minimum habitat areas for cougars using a computer model. According to his findings, if a population is confined to a small area and no immigration of transient lions is possible, the habitat area must be 620–1,370 square miles in size for the population to survive 100 years. Beier cautions that the minimum size is based on an optimistic estimate of lion density. For isolated populations to survive longer than 100 years would require constant monitoring and possible translocation of lions from other populations. For areas smaller than 620 square miles, extinction of the population is almost inevitable. However, if as few as 1 to 4 animals per decade could immigate into a small population, the probability of the population surviving improves greatly. Thus a "corridor" for immigration would benefit a small population in an area where further loss of habitat will occur.[95]

Tying isolated tracts of habitat together with move-ment or conservation corridors is a frequently proposed solution to the rampant habitat fragmentation currently taking place. Larry Harris, an expert on conservation corridors, states that "Our numerous, large wildlife sanctuaries must be made to function as a system, rather than being thought of as islands unto themselves. Physical interconnections of habitat must be developed and safeguarded if the wide-ranging mammals are to survive in perpetuity. In short, we need a system of wildlife conservation corridors to interconnect the many and sometimes large refuges already

APPROXIMATE HOME RANGE NEEDS IN ACRES OF OTTER, BOBCAT, BLACK BEAR, AND FLORIDA PANTHER

In Florida, rampant urban, residential, and agricultural growth has led to extensive wildlife habitat loss and fragmentation. Florida panthers and other animals that require large home ranges, must traverse miles of increasingly hostile landscape, filled with roads, canals, and residential developments (Harris and Gallagher 1989, modified).

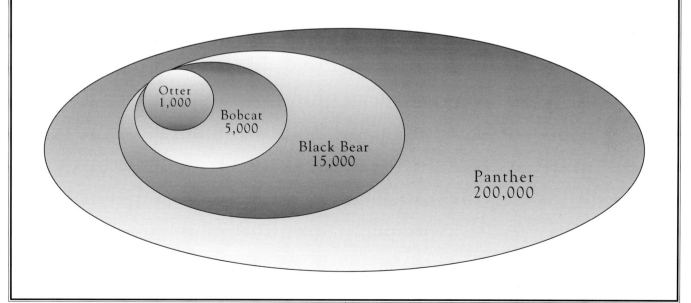

established."[93] New Mexico lion researcher Linda Sweanor emphasizes the importance of wildlife corridors to cougars: "It is apparent that fragmented habitat may only support lions on a long-term basis if individuals are allowed to successfully immigrate, hence requiring dispersal from other local populations. To conserve populations of mountain lions over the long term, adequate habitats must be maintained in an effective patchwork composed of relatively large blocks of wildland reserves interconnected by dispersal corridors."[96]

Beier's research has shown that not only are movement corridors important to the cat's survival, but the cougar is an ideal species for identification of corridor locations. This is because the cougar is an area-sensitive species dependent on the size of its habitat for existence and successful reproduction. Thus, a movement corridor identified on the basis of cougar use is likely to benefit at least one species. Secondly, a hunting cougar travels an average of 5 1/2 miles per night and as a result generates lots of corridor information in a short time. Collection of comparable information for less wide-ranging species may take years or generations.[95]

Protecting and maintaining large tracts of land is crucial to lions as well as other species. The concept of small, isolated areas of habitat connected by movement corridors has a lot of potential, but is still a largely untested theory and should not be considered an alternative to major habitat acquisition. Wildlife corridors will likely prove most valuable in mitigating the effects of a badly fragmented landscape where further loss of wildlife habitat will occur.

Though our past record of wildlife habitat protection is poor, some recent events give cause for hope. First of all, in June 1990, the people of California passed the Wildlife Protection Act of 1990 (Proposition 117). Proposition 117 prohibits trophy hunting of mountain lions, tightens regulations on protection of livestock from lions, and requires the state to spend $30 million annually for the next 30 years to protect wildlife habitat in California. In all, 57,761

acres of wildlife habitat were acquired in the first year under the provisions of this new law. "We are proud to have helped in writing and passing Proposition 117," said Mark J. Palmer, Conservation Director of the Mountain Lion Foundation. "Many exciting natural areas have now been permanently protected by the state for all people to enjoy. Endangered species, mountain lions, deer, wetlands, and riparian (streamside) zones have all benefited from this landmark new law."[97]

Officials in northern Florida are attempting to purchase tracts of land in an effort to create conservation corridors. The recent protective designation of Pinhook Swamp creates a strategic link between the much larger Osceola National Forest and Okeefenokee National Wildlife Refuge. Now the area encompasses sufficient prime habitat that it could be considered as a possible site for the reintroduction of the Florida panther.[91]

In Los Angeles, efforts are underway to protect a wildlife corridor connecting the isolated Santa Monica Mountains with the inland wilderness in Angeles and Los Padres national forests. The corridor, a narrowing swath of land, acts as a crucial habitat link for animals to replenish populations in the urban parklands. Even here, adjacent to the second-largest urban area in the United States, experts estimate a small population of less than 10 cougars survive.[98]

Finally, the northeastern woods are coming back. Forest ecologist Susan Morse, who makes her home in Vermont, explains what is happening: "Today, we are literally watching the land rebuild itself and much of our former wildlife is returning, some with our help of course. This is true in varying degrees throughout the Northeast, but it is especially pronounced in northern New England where human population pressures have not been felt for many decades. Now you can see beaver ponds strung like pearls between clean, flowing streams. Moose, deer, bear, bobcat, river otter, fisher, and fox have returned, along with the coyote, a newcomer to this region. [Some believe the eastern panther itself is back.] New plant growth is slowly repairing what was a ravaged land a mere 80 years ago. It's our second chance at paradise."[88]

Unfortunately, the comeback of the northeastern forests is facing a new threat. Over 85 percent of the roughly 26 million acres of forest land are privately held, mostly by a dozen companies, families, and trusts. Population growth, second-home development, massive clear cutting, and pressures from Wall Street on longtime owners to sell are raising the specter of subdividing the wilderness. Increasingly, the land has less value as timberland than as house lots. In the current depressed economy neither environmental groups nor the federal government has taken any concrete steps towards preservation.[99] This too is unfortunate for, as Susan Morse points out, "It will never get any cheaper or easier to take care of habitat and wildlife than now."[88] Without protective action, this second paradise could become paradise lost—again.

RESEARCH

As has been discussed, cougars are secretive, solitary, and highly mobile carnivores that occur in low densities and roam enormous tracts of wilderness. For decades, these characteristics have made the species extremely difficult to research. The only sources of information about mountain lion populations were observations made and the carcasses collected by professional hunters. Jay Bruce, California's official lion hunter from 1914 to 1942, was one of the first to record anatomical measurements of lions and estimate their home range and population sizes. Not surprisingly, his observations always showed the need for a state-supported lion hunter.[1]

Frank C. Hibben was probably the first biologist to enter the cougar's domain and attempt a scientific examination. He spent a year (1934–1935) accompanying lion hunters throughout New Mexico and Arizona and analyzed the stomach contents of the cougars they killed. Hibben's findings showed deer were the preferred prey and that livestock appeared in only 2 percent of the lions examined. He also considered attaching metal tags to the ears of some lions to learn something of their movements, but soon abandoned the idea. "[I]t was feared that this would raise too much opposition with cattle and game interests."[76]

In 1946, Stanley P. Young and Edward A. Goldman, biologists with U.S. Fish and Wildlife Service, wrote *The Puma: Mysterious American Cat*, the most comprehensive summary of knowledge on cougars up to that time. The book was based primarily on the records of federal trappers working in the West.[7] During the next 15 years, researcher W. Leslie Robinette continued to examine the cougar's food habits in Nevada and Utah, again relying primarily on the stomach contents of lions killed by federal and private hunters. He also wrote about cougar productivity and life history.[100, 101]

The first structured field study of mountain lions was conducted by Maurice Hornocker in the Idaho Primitive Area (now the Frank Church River of No Return Wilderness) in the mid-1960s. Working with veteran lion hunter Wilbur Wiles, Hornocker tracked and treed cougars with dogs, then sedated them with newly developed drugs administered through darts fired from an air rifle. They tracked, treed, weighed, measured, photographed, released, and recaptured dozens of the big cats through several bitter-cold Idaho winters. Hornocker's work was the first ever to use marked mountain lions to document territoriality in any cat species. He was first to recognize and describe the role of "transient" individuals, as opposed to full-time residents in a population, and the ways in which such transients may recolonize adjacent areas. Further, his analysis of the effect of cougar predation on elk and deer populations is regarded as classic.[62, 102]

In the early 1970s, Hornocker and Wiles were joined by researchers John Seidensticker and John Messick.

Several of the cougars in the study area were fitted with radio collars so their movements could be monitored. The radio telemetry work provided important information on the social organization of the lions in the Idaho Primative Area. It also contributed to population estimates, sex, age, reproductive status, and population health data.[61]

Additional studies followed as other researchers adopted Hornocker and Seidensticker's methods and soon more pieces of the puzzle began to fall into place. Cougar research has been conducted in every western state as well as Florida, Alberta, and British Columbia. Harley Shaw's work in Arizona contributed valuable information on livestock depredation and the tracking of lions. Fred Lindzey coordinated the team of biologists on the 10-year Boulder-Escalante Cougar Project in southern Utah, which provided important data on the cat's food habits, habitat use, and response to hunting. Canadian researchers Martin Jalkotsy and Ian Ross are finishing up another 10-year study in Alberta, and Paul Beier's work in southern California may help save a threatened population of pumas from rampant habitat loss. In Florida, researchers such as David Maehr, Sonny Bass, and Chris Belden are fighting to save the endangered panther.

Today, as founder and director of the Wildlife Research Institute, Hornocker and his hand-picked teams of biologists are engaged in a 10-year study of cougars and their prey in the desert environment of New Mexico and a comprehensive ecological study of cougars in Yellowstone National Park.[103] (Both of these studies were mentioned previously.) Hornocker's almost 30 years of experience studying different cougar populations in a variety of habitats provides valuable insight into the variability of lion behavior.

Though many questions have been answered, many more questions remain. Information is lacking in a large portion of the cougar's range, particularly in Mexico and Central and South America. Wildlife managers and researchers still search for better ways to census and estimate population sizes, better sexing and aging techniques, ways to estimate population growth, ways to determine the impact of hunting on populations, and nonlethal ways to reduce livestock depredation. In many cases, basic survival information—such as the size of populations, the size of habitats, and the number of kittens that survive to adulthood—is lacking.

In 1988, Lynne Trulio, an ecologist formerly with the Mountain Lion Foundation, conducted a survey of 30 mountain lion experts throughout the United States and Canada, gathering the opinions of experts on research methods and perhaps helping guide scientists as they design their studies. Trulio concluded: "Respondents listed the three primary problems with research today as funding, study length/intensity, and methodology problems...These problems all impede the understanding of mountain lions and prevent us from addressing the threats which face this species."[104]

Allen Anderson, in his comprehensive review of literature on the mountain lion, made the following recommendations regarding research needs: "Aside from the diet and certain variables of reproductive biology,...it is not possible to generalize on any aspect of puma biology. Thus, research is needed on all aspects. However, I believe research having a direct bearing on the welfare of puma should receive first priority. Since sport hunting is the major and only controllable source of recorded puma mortality, I suggest research on the effects of sport hunting on specific puma populations should receive that priority. Second priority should be concerned with...census and aging techniques...."[105]

Few research studies have monitored cougar populations over periods longer than a few years, and experts are reluctant to apply findings to cougar populations in different areas, given the cat's recognized adaptability and subsequent behavioral variation. Lack of standardized research methods make it difficult for researchers to share and apply information. As a result, wildlife administrators too frequently face the task of designing cougar management programs based on research data that is both scant and questionable.

MANAGEMENT

It is Aldo Leopold's 1933 book, *Game Management*, that is generally recognized as the birth of the science of game management,[106] though many of its professionals acknowledge that the discipline is still so young that it is more an art than a science. Early game-management philosophy was similar to that of agriculture, and in many ways is still practiced today. Killing of game is a "harvest" and a population of animals a "crop." The most common approach in most agencies responsible for game management is a technique called "sustained-yield harvesting." Ordinarily, this involves killing a "surplus" portion of a population at a rate that balances the productivity in that population.[40] Since almost all game managers depend on hunting license purchases as their primary source of revenue, the focus of management is usually on maximizing populations for the benefit of hunters. As a result, the partnership between the hunting community and game managers has a long tradition, and the influence of the hunting community has on game management practices is substantial. In many cases game populations are not managed *by* hunting, as is so often claimed; rather, populations are managed *for* hunting. Under such circumstances, politics frequently play a bigger role in management decisions than does biology.

Today, the cougar is trapped in the crossfire of conflicting management goals. Management goals may vary from the reestablishment of viable populations in their former range, as found in the Florida Panther Recovery Plan, to the complexity of maintaining viable cougar populations while providing hunting opportunities and reducing livestock losses[41] in Idaho, to complete protection of the cougar in California. While the wildlife management responsibility of most agencies ends at the state line, lions frequently cross them. A protected cougar in California that crosses into Nevada becomes a game animal. Yet, there is little coordination in management or research between states or provinces. Agencies even maintain their records differently. (For instance, collecting and reconciling the sport-hunting statistics for this book was a long and arduous task.)

There is little evidence that sport hunting is of any benefit to cougar populations. Nor does hunting protect deer herds, decrease depredation, or reduce the risk of attacks on people. Under such circumstances hunting advocates find themselves in the position of trying to prove sport hunting does not "harm" lion populations. The biological jury is still out on this question, but considering our past record in predator management it seems wise to err to the side of caution. A mountain lion's hide is of little value and its meat is rarely eaten. The primary justification for hunting mountain lions is because hunters want to collect a trophy.

However, in a national survey conducted by the U.S. Fish and Wildlife Service, 80 percent of the American people disapproved of trophy hunting.[107] Former California Governor George Deukmejian, the California Fish and Game Commission, and the Department of Fish and Game (DFG) all underestimated this change in attitude toward wildlife, particularly mountain lions. In 1985, Deukmejian vetoed a hunting moratorium on mountain lions that had been in place since 1972. The commission and DFG subsequently recommended a sport hunt. A coalition of conservation groups were able to stop the hunt for five years through court action. But the most dramatic public statement came on June 6, 1990, when the people of California approved ballot initiative Proposition 117 which permanently banned mountain lion hunting in the state.

Increasing environmental awareness, concern over loss

of habitat, and evolving attitudes toward animals has a new generation of wildlife biologists advocating a shift from "game management" to "wildlife management." "A sense of profound change pervades the wildlife management field today," writes Stephen R. Kellert.[108] "Various indicators suggest that basic shifts have occurred in American attitudes and recreational uses of wildlife. These changes have been reflected, for example, in a series of studies of American attitudes, knowledge, and behaviors toward wildlife[107,109,110] as well as in the findings of the 1980 National hunting, fishing, and wildlife-related recreation survey,[111] which estimated that a remarkable $40 billion [is] spent on all forms of wildlife recreation, including $14.8 billion on nonconsumptive wildlife use." Nonconsumptive wildlife use includes such activities as birdwatching, visits to zoos or museums, scientific study, or photography.[107]

Many state wildlife agencies are being called upon to expand their responsibilities beyond traditional game management into such areas as nongame management, nature education, and environmental protection and mitigation. There are those who feel wildlife agencies should be spending more time managing the 90 percent of animal species that are not hunted, as well as acquiring and protecting critical habitat for nongame and game. Unfortunately, these new demands come at a time of tight budgets and declining revenues from hunting and fishing licenses, revenues that provide a large portion of the operating capital for many state wildlife agencies.

Nowhere is this dilemma better represented than in California. A recent study of the California Department of Fish and Game (DFG) by the Legislative Analyst's Office[112] made the following observation: "DFG historically has provided services and programs primarily for those that use or consume the state's wildlife and natural habitat resource, such as individuals who hunt and fish. As California's population has grown, leading to increasing urbanization, this traditional constituency group of the

DFG has diminished steadily. Meanwhile, the responsibilities of the DFG relating to general habitat protection and endangered species protection have increased, requiring the DFG to expand services and programs that protect the overall resource base. What is lacking, however, is a clear focus on exactly what the DFG's relative priorities are...." The report makes a number of recommendations to the State Legislature to resolve ongoing problems within DFG. At the top of the list is: "Determine the primary mission of the department so that conflicts between programs focused on resource use and programs focused on resource protection can be resolved."[112]

Our current wildlife habitat crisis makes it imperative that we also shift our management emphasis from "species" to "spaces." For instance, few cougar management programs are coordinated with deer management, yet deer are the primary food source for the cats and suffer the same consequences of habitat loss. The future of both species is irrevocably linked, while at the same time their interactions are poorly understood. The extensive data being assembled by scientists about mule deer could prove valuable in cougar management as well. Detailed maps of the summer and winter ranges of migratory deer herds could provide a good template for preliminary identification of cougar habitat. Inventories of preferred forage for deer and the location of kills made by cougars could add to the limited information available on the favored stalking cover of the big cats. Such "integrated management" would be beneficial to the many other plant and animal species found within deer and mountain lion habitat.

In a 1983 report to the New Mexico State Legislature, Wain Evans, assistant director of the State Game and Fish Department, recommended that the best approach to cougar management was to allow populations to stabilize and to reimburse ranchers for the few losses to cats. Evans states in his report that "The cougar's biology render their populations uniquely unsusceptible to most forms of wildlife management. Efforts to reduce depredations on live-stock and wildlife through cougar hunting and control on problem areas have failed. While of biological origin, depredations of livestock are essentially a political concern. Cougar management should recognize that present know-how and technologies are not sufficient to artificially cali-brate cougar populations short of extirpation. Management should take advantage of the cougar's self-limiting potential by allowing development of stable social structures over most of the occupied range...a system of reimbursing ranch-ers for at least part of their loss should be developed."[32]

It is time wildlife managers look to the cougar as more than a revenue-generating game animal or a pest that occa-sionally preys on livestock. Kellert reminds us that "If the wildlife profession is to avoid increasing isolation from the millions of Americans primarily interested in non-game wildlife, dramatic changes in traditional programs will be required."[108] As the wildlife manager's constituency expands and diversifies, he can expect management deci-sions to be subject to even greater scrutiny. Fred Lindzey points out that, "It is easier to quantify the dollar value of livestock losses than the recreational and esthetics values associated with mountain lions." He warns that manage-ment programs that provide for sport hunting and the killing of cougars to protect livestock will be exposed to increasing scrutiny in the future, and that "Management agencies must be prepared to document that such removals will not result in a loss of the population."[41]

A PERSONAL PERSPECTIVE

Finally, coexistence with cougars is possible, but it requires changing our attitude toward the wild animals that share our landscape. Living in cougar country poses some risk, but it's a manageable one. Part of Florida's success in bring-ing the alligator back from the brink of extinction was an aggressive public education campaign about the importance of making room for wildlife. Both the Colorado Division of Wildlife and the Montana Department of Fish, Wildlife and Parks have produced excellent brochures on how to live with mountain lions, and the Mountain Lion Foundation works hard to get the facts out about cougars. Renowned puma biologist Stanley Young once said, "The almost universal fear of the puma is based mainly on its mysterious ways, size, and power to do harm, not on its aggressiveness, for as a rule it is notoriously timid in rela-tion to man."[7] Perhaps it's time for man to give a little.

Chapter 5. Cougars and Humans (Notes)

1. Acuff, D.S. 1988. Perceptions of the mountain lion, 1825–1986, with emphasis on *Felis concolor californica*. M.A. thesis, University of California, Davis.

2. Hodge, G.M. 1967. *The kachinas are coming: Pueblo Indian kachina dolls with related folk tales*. Northland Press, Flagstaff, Arizona. (Cited from Acuff 1988.)

3. Parsons, E.C. 1936. *Taos Pueblo*. Banta Publishing Co., Menasha, Wisconsin (Cited from Acuff 1988.)

4. Harrington, J.P. 1916. Ethnogeography of the Tewa Indians, *Bureau of American Ethnology annual report*, Vol. 29 (1916), pp. 29–636. Washington, D.C. (Cited from Acuff 1988.)

5. Alexander, H.B. 1916. *The mythology of all races: North America*. Cambridge: Cambridge University Press. (Cited from Acuff 1988.)

6. Montijo, Y. 1990. The story of the mountain lion. *News From Native California*, Spring 1990: 56.

7. Young, S.P. and E.A. Goldman. 1946. *The puma: Mysterious American cat*. American Wildlife Institute, Washington, D.C.

8. Newcomb, F.J. 1965. Origin of the Navajo eagle chant. In *Journal of American Folklore*, Vol. 53 (1965), pp. 50–77. (Cited from Acuff 1988.)

9. Saxton, D.F. and L. Saxton. 1973. *O'othham hoho'ok a'githa: Legends and lore of the Papago and Pima Indians*. University of Arizona Press, Tucson. (Cited from Acuff 1988.)

10. Lange, C.H. 1959. *Cochiti: A New Mexican pueblo past and present*. University of Texas Press, Austin. (Cited from Acuff 1988.)

11. Parsons, E.C. 1939. *Pueblo Indian religion*. University of Chicago Press, Chicago. (Cited from Acuff 1988.)

12. White, L.A. 1942. *The pueblo of Santa Ana, New Mexico*. Memoirs of the American Anthropological Association, Vol. 60. (Cited from Acuff 1988.)

13. Turbak, G. and A. Carey. 1986. *America's great cats*. Northland Publishing, Flagstaff, Arizona.

14. Tinsley, J.B. 1987. *The puma: Legendary lion of the Americas*. Texas Western Press, The University of Texas at El Paso.

15. Steinhardt, P. 1989. Taming our fear of predators. *National Wildlife*, February/March: 4–12.

16. Grey, Z. 1922. *Tales of the lonely trails*. Blue Ribbon Books, New York. (Cited from Acuff 1988.)

17. Spargo, J. 1950. *The catamount in Vermont*. Bennington, Vermont.

18. Laycock, G. 1988. Cougars in conflict. *Audubon*. March: 86–95.

19. Eaton, E. 1987. Man and the cougar: images of an outlaw. Pages 12–13 in K. Springer, ed. *Biologue: A journal of interpretation and discovery in the life sciences*. Teton Science School, Kelly, Wyoming.

20. Satchell, M. and J.M. Schorf. 1990. Uncle Sam's war on wildlife. *U.S. News and World Report*. February 5: 36–37.

21. Predator control: Death as a way of life. 1971. *Environmental Action*, 21 August 1971.

22. Schneider, K. 1991. Big federal hunts of predators may backfire, biologists warn. *The Sacramento Bee*, 9 June 1991.

23. Armentrout, D. 1984. Toward a national predator policy. Paper presented at National Audubon Society, Western Regional Conference, Asilomar, California.

24. Phelps, J.S. 1989. Status of mountain lions in Arizona. Pages 7–9 in R.H. Smith, ed. *Proceedings of the third mountain lion workshop*, Prescott, Arizona.

25. Anderson, A.E. and R.J. Tully. 1989. Status of the mountain lion in Colorado. Pages 19–23 in R.H. Smith, ed. *Proceedings of the third mountain lion workshop*, Prescott, Arizona.

26. Nowak, R.M. 1976. *The cougar in the United States and Canada*. New York Zoological Society and U.S. Fish and Wildlife Service Office of Endangered Species, Washington, D.C.

27. Hebert, D. 1989. The status and management of cougar in British Columbia 1988. Pages 11–14 in R.H. Smith, ed. *Proceedings of the third mountain lion workshop*, Prescott, Arizona.

28. Shaw, H.G. 1989. *Soul among lions*. Johnson Books. Boulder, Colorado.

29. Thompson, R.A. 1992. State Director, U.S. Department of Agriculture, Animal and Plant Health Inspection Service, Animal Damage Control. Sacramento, California. (Personal communication)

30. U.S. Department of Agriculture. 1990. Animal and Plant Health Inspection Service. *Animal damage control program, draft environmental impact statement-1990*.

31. California Department of Fish and Game. 1988. *Mountain lion depredation summary statewide*. Sacramento.

32. Evans, W. 1983. *The cougar in New Mexico: Biology, status, depredation of livestock, and management recommendations*. New Mexico Department of Fish and Game, Santa Fe.

33. Suminski, H.R. 1982. Mountain lion predation on domestic livestock in Nevada. *Proceedings of the vertebrate pest conference*. 10:62–66.

34. Lindzey, F.G. 1991. Wildlife Biologist, U.S. Fish and Wildlife Service, Wyoming Cooperative Fish and Wildlife Research Unit, University of Wyoming, Laramie, Wyoming. (Personal communication)

35. Trulio, L. 1989a. *Livestock depredation: Why lions are not a major threat to California's livestock industry.* Pouncing on the myths about mountain lions, Volume IV, Mountain Lion Preservation Foundation Series, Sacramento, California.

36. Bowns, J.E. 1985. Predation-depredation. Pages 204–215 *in* J. Roberson and F.G. Lindzey, eds. *Proceedings of the second mountain lion workshop*, Salt Lake City, Utah.

37. Hopkins, R.A. 1989. Ecology of the puma in the Diablo Range, California. Ph.D. dissertation, University of California at Berkeley.

38. Shaw, H. 1987. *Mountain lion field guide*. 3rd Edition. Special Report Number 9. Arizona Game and Fish Department.

39. de Treville, S. 1991. Wildlife Biologist. de Treville Environmental Engineering. San Diego, California. (Personal communication)

40. Dixon, K.R. 1982. Mountain lion. Pages 711–727 *in* J.A. Chapman and G.A. Feldhamer, eds. *Wild mammals of North America*. John Hopkins University Press. Baltimore.

41. Lindzey, F. 1987. Mountain lion. Pages 656–668 *in* M. Novak, J.A. Baker, M.E. Obbard, and B. Malloch, eds. *Wild furbearer management and conservation in North America*. Ministry of Natural Resources, Ontario, Canada.

42. Hopkins, R.A. 1992. Wildlife Biologist, H.T. Harvey and Associates, Alviso, California. (Personal communication)

43. Leyhausen, P. 1979. *Cat behavior: The predatory and social behavior of domestic and wild cats.* Garland STPM Press, New York. Translated by B.A. Tomkin.

44. Kitchener, A. 1991. *The natural history of the wild cats*. Cornell University Press.

45. Guggisberg, C.A.W. 1975. *Wild cats of the world*. Taplinger Publishing Co., New York.

46. Lindzey, F.G., B.B. Ackerman, D. Barnhurst, T. Becker, T.P. Hemker, S.P. Laing, C. Mecham, and W.D. Van Sickle. 1989. *Boulder-Escalante cougar project final report*. Utah. Division of Wildlife Resources, Salt Lake City, Utah.

47. U.S. Fish and Wildlife Service. 1979. *Ranchers say electric fencing protects sheep from coyotes*. Denver Wildlife Research Center, Denver, Colorado.

48. Green, J.S. 1981. Reducing coyote damage to sheep with non-lethal techniques. *Proceedings of the fifth Great Plains wildlife damage control workshop*, Lincoln, Nebraska.

49. Sibbison, H.R. 1984. So sheep may safely graze. *Defenders*:11–19.

50. Dagget, D. 1988. Dishonorable discharges. *New Times*. August:18–23.

51. Connolly, G.E. 1978. Predators and predator control. Pages 369–394 *in* J.L. Schmidt and D.L. Gilbert, eds. *Big game of North America: Ecology and management*. Wildlife Management Institute. Stackpole Books.

52. Errington, P.L. 1967. *Of predation and life*. Iowa State University Press, Ames.

53. Lindzey, F.G., B.B. Ackerman, D. Barnhurst, and T.P. Hemker. 1988. Survival rates of mountain lions in southern Utah. *Journal of Wildlife Management*, 52:664–667.

54. Murphy, K. 1983. *Characteristics of a hunted population of mountain lions in western Montana. (Relationships between a mountain lion population and hunting pressure in western Montana.)* Report to the Montana Department of Fish, Wildlife and Parks.

55. Ashman, D., G.C. Christensen, M.L. Hess, G.K. Tsukamoto, and M.S. Wickersham. 1983. *The mountain lion in Nevada*. Nevada Department of Wildlife, Reno.

56. Lindzey, F.G., W.D. Van Sickle, S.P. Laing, and C.S. Mecham. 1992. Simulated cougar harvest in southern Utah. *Journal of Wildlife Management*, In Press.

57. Streubel, D. 1990. Mountain lion under study in Idaho. *Northern Rockies Conservation Cooperative News*, Jackson, Wyoming Summer: 8.

58. Barnhurst, D.E. 1986. Vulnerability of cougars to hunting. M.S. Thesis, Utah State University, Logan.

59. Hemker, T.P., F.G. Lindzey, B.B. Ackerman, and A.J. Button. 1986. Survival of cougar cubs in a nonhunted population. Page 327–332 *in* S.D. Miller and D.D. Everett, eds. *Cats of the world: Biology, conservation and management*. Proceedings of the Second International Cat Symposium. Caesare Kleberg Wildlife Research Institute. Kingsville, Texas.

60. Logan, K.A. 1991. Wildlife Research Institute, Inc., Moscow, Idaho. (Personal communication)

61. Seidensticker, J.C., IV, M.G. Hornocker, W.V. Wiles, and J.P. Messick. 1973. Mountain lion social organization in the Idaho Primitive Area. *Wildlife Monographs*, 35.

62. Hornocker, M.G. 1970. An analysis of mountain lion predation upon mule deer and elk in the Idaho Primitive Area. *Wildlife Monographs*, 21:1–39.

63. Akeman, T. 1991a. Rancher tells why big cats were killed. *The Monterey Herald*, 26 April 1991.

64. Schrader, E. 1991. Big-game hunting organizers convicted. *San Jose Mercury News*, 26 June 1991.

65. Moreno, E.M. 1991. 'Big-cat' case jury convicts couple. *The Monterey Herald*, 26 June 1991.

66. Glick, D. 1990. The new killing fields. *Newsweek*, July 23, 1990: 54–55.

67. Milstein, M. 1989. The quiet kill. *National Parks*, May/June 1989:19–24.

68. Poten, C.J. 1991. A shameful harvest: America's illegal wildlife trade. *National Geographic*, September 1991.

69. Farnsworth, C.L. 1980. A descriptive analysis of the extent of commercial poaching in the United States. Ph.D. dissertation, Sam Houston State University, Huntsville, Texas.

70. Reisner, M. 1987. Bad news, bears. *California Magazine*, March: 71–128.

71. California Senate Office of Research Issue Brief. 1987. *The crime of poaching*. August.

72. Swendsen, D.H. 1985. *Badge in the wilderness: My 30 dangerous years combating wildlife violators*. Stackpole Books, Harrisburg, Pennsylvania.

73. Bontadelli, P. 1991. Former Director, California Department of Fish and Game. Sacramento, California. (Personal communication)

74. Akeman, T. 1991b. Rancher gets jail, fine in big-cat case. *The Monterey Herald*, 17 August 1991.

75. Storer, T.I. 1923. Rabies in a mountain lion. *California Fish and Game*, April 9(2):45–48.

76. Hibben, F.C. 1937. *A preliminary study of the mountain lion (Felis oregonensis [sub] sp.)*. The University of New Mexico Bulletin. Biological Series 5(3):1–59.

77. Mills, E. 1922. *Watched by wild animals*. New York: Doubleday. (Cited From Acuff 1988.)

78. Garnass, S. and M. Robinson. 1991. Lion suspected in jogger death. *The Denver Post*, 17 January 1991.

79. Beier, P. 1991. Cougar attacks on humans in the United States and Canada. *Wildlife Society Bulletin*, 19:403–412.

80. Pemble, D. 1991. Wildlife Control Officer, Province of British Columbia, Ministry of Environment and Parks, Conservation Officer Service, Abbotsford, British Columbia. (Personal communication)

81. Seidensticker, J.C. and S. Lumpkin. 1992. Mountain lions don't stalk people. True or false? *Smithsonian*, February:113–122.

82. Bensimhon, D. and M. Brophy. 1992. Man-killers. *Men's Health*, April:79.

83. Sacks, J.J., R.W. Satin, and S.E. Bonzo. 1989. Dog bite fatalities from 1979 through 1988. *Journal of the American Medical Association*, 262:1489–1492. (Cited from Beier 1991.)

84. Weiss, R. 1990. Researchers foresee antivenin improvements. *Science News*, 138:360–362. (Cited from Beier 1991.)

85. Shaw, H.G. 1991. Wildlife Biologist, General Wildlife Services, Chino Valley, Arizona. (Personal communication)

86. Lait, M. 1991. $2 Million awarded to girl mauled by mountain lion. *Los Angeles Times*, 24 August 1991.

87. Horan, A. 1992b. Adults-only park rule draws criticism. *The Orange County Register*, 7 February 1992.

88. Morse, S.C. 1991. Forest Ecologist and Wildlife Habitat Consultant. Morse and Morse Forestry. Jericho, Vermont. (Personal communication)

89. Van Dyke, F.G., R.H. Brocke, H.G. Shaw, B.B. Ackerman, T.P. Hemker, and F.G. Lindzey. 1986. Reactions of mountain lions to logging and human activity. *Journal of Wildlife Management*, 50(1):95–102.

90. Roberts, R. 1990. There is no turning back: Instincts of deer lead them across roads, where they lose escape skills. *Los Angeles Times*, 31 October 1990.

91. Harris, L.D. and P.B. Gallagher. 1989. New initiatives for wildlife conservation: The need for movement corridors. Pages 11–34 *in* Gay Mackintosh, ed. *Preserving communities and corridors*. Defenders of Wildlife, Washington, D.C.

92. Horan, A. 1992a. 6 cougars were hit on OC roads in '91, study says. *The Orange County Register*, 24 January 1992.

93. Harris, L.D. 1985. Conservation corridors: A highway system for wildlife. *ENFO*, November.

94. Newmark, W.D. 1986. Species-area relationship and its determinants for mammals in western North American national parks. *Biological Journal of the Linnean Society* 28: 83–98.

95. Beier, P. 1992a. Determining minimum habitat areas and habitat corridors for cougars. *Conservation Biology* 6:In Press.

96. Sweanor, L.L. 1990. Mountain lion social organization in a desert environment. M.S. thesis, University of Idaho, Moscow.

97. Palmer, M.J. 1992. CEO/Conservation Director, Mountain Lion Foundation, Sacramento, California. (Personal communication)

98. Edelman, P. 1990. *Critical wildlife corridor/habitat linkage areas between the Santa Susanna Mountains, the Simi Hills and the Santa Monica Mountains.* Prepared for the Nature Conservancy. The Santa Monica Mountains Conservancy. Malibu, California.

99. Austin, P. 1991. Who owns the wilderness in the northern forest? *The Sacramento Bee,* 10 July 1991.

100. Robinette, W.L., J.S. Gashwiler, and O.W. Morris. 1959. Food habits of the cougar in Utah and Nevada. *Journal of Wildlife Management* 23:261–273.

101. ———. 1961. Notes on cougar productivity and life history. *Journal of Mammalogy* 42:204–217.

102. Hornocker, M.G. 1969a. Winter territoriality in mountain lions. *Journal of Wildlife Management* 33:457-464.

103. ———. 1992. Founder and Director, Wildlife Research Institute, Inc., Moscow, Idaho. (Personal communication)

104. Trulio, L. 1989b. What mountain lion scientists say about their research: Results of a survey on mountain lion research methods. Mountain Lion Preservation Foundation, Sacramento, California.

105. Anderson, A.E. 1983. *A critical review of literature on puma (Felis concolor).* Colorado Division of Wildlife. Special Report Number 54.

106. Leopold, A. 1933. *Game management.* The University of Wisconsin Press, Madison, Wisconsin.

107. Kellert, S.R. 1980. *Activities of the American public relating to animals.* U.S. Government Printing Office # 024-010-00-624-2, Washington, D.C.

108. ———. 1985. Birdwatching in American Society. *Leisure Sciences* 7(3):343–360.

109. ———. 1979. *Public attitudes toward critical wildlife and natural habitat issues.* U.S. Government Printing Office # 024-010-00-623-4, Washington, D.C. (Cited from Kellert 1985.)

110. ——— and J.K. Berry. 1981. *Knowledge, affection and basic attitudes toward animals in American society.* U.S. Government Printing Office # 024-010-00-625-1, Washington, D.C. (Cited from Kellert 1985.)

111. U.S. Department of the Interior. 1982. *1980 National Hunting, Fishing and Wildlife-Related Recreation Survey.* Washington, D.C. (Cited from Kellert 1985.)

112. Hill, E.G. 1991. *A review of the Department of Fish and Game: Issues and options for improving its performance.* Legislative Analyst's Office. Sacramento, California. 3 September, 1991.

THE COUGAR IS ENDANGERED: TRUE OR FALSE?

THE ANSWER YOU GET WHEN YOU INQUIRE about the status of the cougar depends largely on who you ask. Research biologists tend to restrict their comments to a particular study area or to one population of cats. State and provincial wildlife managers rarely look beyond their political boundaries when considering a species' status. Federal wildlife biologists will discuss the situation in western North America or in Florida. While these localized perspectives are understandable, they inhibit comprehensive evaluation of the status of mountain lions throughout their range. Things become even more complicated where the cougar's range crosses international boundaries. Everyone involved in cougar management acknowledges the paucity of information about the cats outside temperate North America and this obviously makes it difficult to assess the species' status in the Western Hemisphere.

Compared to the status of cougar populations at the turn of the century—when most states still paid bounties—they certainly seem to have made a comeback in many parts of western North America. On the other hand, the cougar has been displaced from two-thirds of its historical range in temperate North America and scant information exists regarding the cat's status in Mexico, Central, and South America.[1] When examined in this geographic context the status of mountain lions is very much in question.

It is also important to differentiate between the *legal* status of an animal and its *biological* status. Legal status is the level of protection an animal receives under state or federal law. For instance, Montana classifies the cougar as a game animal that may be killed in limited numbers during specified seasons; Texas lists the mountain lion as a non-protected nongame animal that may be killed throughout the year and in unlimited numbers; under California law, the cougar is a specially protected mammal and all hunting is prohibited; the Florida panther is listed as an endangered species and given complete protection under both state and federal law. Biological status refers to the actual biological condition of cougar populations within a state, province, or region, an evaluation usually based on population numbers or trends. Considering how difficult cougars are to count, some question whether the legal status of an animal reflects its true biological status. Wildlife managers can expect this question to be raised more frequently as concern grows over habitat loss and its impact on wildlife numbers.

An accurate assessment of the biological status of cougars in North America would be an arduous and expensive task, and the results subject to broad interpretation. Substantial biological and political obstacles stand in the way of such a survey, many of which have been previously described: the lions' low-density populations and stealthy behavior; the lack of reliable censusing and aging techniques; differing wildlife management goals and priorities; lack of funds and personnel; different approaches to information gathering and record keeping; and lack of coordination at the state, provincial, and national levels.

Wildlife managers consider information from a variety of sources when evaluating lion population numbers and trends: reports from mountain lion hunters, lions killed during collisions with motor vehicles, attacks on livestock, and reported sightings. More sophisticated techniques include *track transecting*, *radio telemetry*, and *computer models*. Track transecting involves driving or walking along dirt roads, systematically searching for mountain lion tracks, which are then carefully measured and recorded. Radio telemetry is the most expensive approach; small radio transmitters are attached to captured lions, whose movements are then regularly monitored and recorded on topographic maps. In computer modeling, various field data are fed into a mathematical program in order to predict what a particular lion population will do under different circumstances. Some of these techniques can be valuable in estimating population trends, but most vary in accuracy and are open to multiple interpretations.

With these considerations in mind, let's examine the status of cougars in three regions of North America: the West, the Southeast, and the Northeast.

THE WEST

Some biologists consider the cougar to be rebounding in western North America. The reasons most frequently cited are the elimination of bounties, more restrictive hunting regulations, and the preservation of large tracts of public land; however, most biologists are reluctant to give specific numbers, given the difficulty of counting the individuals in even one population.

U.S. Fish and Wildlife Service biologist Ronald Nowak conducted one of the most comprehensive cougar assessments in the United States and Canada in the early 1970s; his one-year general survey (between 1973 and 1974) consisted primarily of a literature review and interviews with biologists and wildlife managers throughout the states and provinces of North America. Nowak summarized his findings for the West: "Presently there is a general consensus in the West that, while far from perfect, regulatory measures have allowed cougar populations to stabilize or even to recover in most states."[2] During the Third Mountain Lion Workshop in Prescott, Arizona (1988), biologists reported that cougar populations had increased in British Columbia,[3] California,[4] Colorado,[5] Nevada,[6] Texas,[7] and Wyoming.[8] Paul Beier stated that: "Although other states have not estimated population trend,[9] cougar populations throughout the West probably increased during 1965–1980 as each state and province changed the legal status of the cougar from bountied predator to game species subject to controlled hunting or (in California) full protection."[10]

While such progress is encouraging, there is another aspect to the cougar's western comeback. Three western subspecies, although not listed as threatened or endangered, have disappeared from over half their former range.

F. c. stanleyana, which formerly occupied most of Texas and Oklahoma, is now restricted to eastern New Mexico and western Texas. Surprisingly, two of the cats were recently killed in east Texas, far from what is considered to be their current range. As the reader may recall, cougars have little protection under current Texas laws, nor do they receive any federal protection; they are considered "varmints" and can be shot or trapped anytime and in unlimited numbers. But even in this traditional stronghold, attitudes are changing. The Lone Star Chapter of the

Sierra Club recently filed a petition with the Texas Parks and Wildlife Department asking the department to declare the mountain lion a protected nongame animal. This would prohibit killing or capturing a cougar without a state permit, unless the animal was attacking someone.[11] The Texas Parks and Wildlife Regulation Committee met in January 1992 and reviewed the status of mountain lions in Texas. While agreeing to sponsor and conduct a roundtable workshop on mountain lion management and research needs in Texas, the committee refused to change the cougar's current classification as a nonprotected nongame species.[12]

F.c. missoulensis and *F.c. hippolestes* are also now restricted to the western portion of larger ranges that once included the northern and central plains, respectively, (see map, page 6).However, sightings still occur in Kansas[13] and South Dakota's Black Hills,[14] and a cougar was shot by a deer hunter in the Nebraska Panhandle in November of 1991.[15] The possibility that some of these are escaped captive cougars cannot be discounted.

The Yuma puma (*Felis concolor browni*) is a subspecies that lives in the desert and riparian habitats along the lower Colorado River in California, Arizona, and Mexico. It has been described as smaller, paler, and of a more yellowish coat than neighboring lions. While there is considerable disagreement over whether it merits recognition as a subspecies, there is no question that the population is in trouble—damming of the Colorado River and adjacent agricultural development has lead to a decline in the habitat of the desert mule deer, the Yuma puma's primary prey. Listed by the U.S. Fish and Wildlife Service as a candidate species for endangered status (Category 2) in December 1982, it was later recognized as a species of special concern by the California Department of Fish and Game in 1986. The California DFG recommended protection of the subspecies, field studies and protection of riparian habitats along the Colorado River.[16] The Arizona Game and

LEGAL STATUS* OF COUGARS IN CANADA AND THE UNITED STATES

CANADA

British Columbia	Game	Manitoba	Protected
Alberta	Game	Ontario	Unprotected
Northwest Territories	Unprotected	Quebec	Protected
Yukon	Unprotected	New Brunswick	Endangered
Saskatchewan	Protected	Nova Scotia	Endangered

UNITED STATES

Montana	Game	Kentucky	Protected
Wyoming	Game	Missouri	Endangered
Idaho	Game	Oklahoma	Protected
Washington	Game	Arkansas	Protected
Oregon	Game	Louisiana	Protected
California	Protected	Mississippi	Endangered
Nevada	Game	Alabama	Protected
Utah	Game	Georgia	Protected
Colorado	Game	South Carolina	Protected
Arizona	Game	North Carolina	Protected
New Mexico	Game	Tennessee	Endangered
Texas	Unprotected	Virginia	Protected
Florida	Endangered	West Virginia	Protected
Alaska	Unprotected	Maryland	Endangered
North Dakota	Unprotected	Delaware	Endangered
South Dakota	Protected	Pennsylvania	Unprotected
Nebraska	Unprotected	New Jersey	Endangered
Kansas	Protected	New York	Endangered
Iowa	Unprotected	Connecticut	Protected
Minnesota	Unprotected	Rhode Island	Extirpated
Wisconsin	Unprotected	Massachusetts	Protected
Michigan	Unprotected	Vermont	Endangered
Ohio	Extirpated	New Hampshire	Endangered
Indiana	Extirpated	Maine	Extirpated
Illinois	Endangered		

*This table applies to laws at the state and provincial level only. The Eastern panther (*F. c. couguar*) and Florida panther (*F. c. coryi*) are protected under the federal Endangered Species Act (ESA) within their historical ranges in the eastern United States. Canada has no comparable law at the national level.

Sources: Nowak 1976, Deems and Pursley 1978, Tully 1991, state and provincial wildlife departments throughout the United States and Canada.

Fish Department considers the Yuma puma endangered, and it appears on the 1988 list of *Threatened Native Wildlife in Arizona.*[17]

Farther west, in the Santa Monica Mountains of Los Angeles County, a tiny population of mountain lions hangs on. Estimated at only 5 to 12 resident members, this population survives in the increasingly fragmented landscape that lies adjacent to one of the largest urban areas in the United States. (This population of lions belongs to the subspecies *Felis concolor californica*, which is found throughout California.) While much of the land in the mountain range is owned and managed by federal, state, and county conservation agencies, rampant development on private land increasingly isolates these fragile islands of wildlife habitat. The Santa Monica Mountains Conservancy and other government agencies are working to acquire land corridors in order to maintain the critical connections between tracts of protected land within the mountain range.

Unfortunately, a more ominous threat looms. Urban and residential growth may isolate the entire Santa Monica Mountain Range from the inland wilderness of the Angeles and Los Padres national forests, which will make it impossible for mountain lions, and many other animals, to immigrate into the mountain range and enhance the resident populations.[18]

In early 1988, Sean Manion, a conservation biologist with the Topanga-Las Virgenes Resource Conservation District, petitioned the U.S. Fish and Wildlife Service to place the Santa Monica Mountains cougar population on the federal Endangered Species List. Later the same year, the petition was refused; USFWS cited inadequate information (no formal study of the lion population in the Santa Monica Mountains has ever been done) and the lack of evidence that the lions even represented a distinct population. They also stated that while extensive habitat loss was occurring, it was not considered to be affecting a significant portion of the lion's entire range, which includes all of California.[19] This finding was particularly disturbing in light of the fact that most habitat loss is incremental in nature.

Just down the freeway from the Santa Monica Mountains is the Santa Ana Mountain Range, a series of smaller mountains that border the eastern side of Orange County, where the rate of urban growth outpaces even that of Los Angeles. Since 1987, the mountain lion population in the Santa Ana Mountains has been under the scrutiny of Paul Beier. (These cats are also classified *F. c. californica.*) Thirty-two cougars have been radio-collared and Beier estimates that the population consists of 10 to 14 adult females, 4 adult males, and 10 to 20 juveniles. While the cats generally seem healthy, the increasing isolation of the mountain range worries Beier. Of particular concern are two wildlife movement corridors, one at each end of the mountain range, that are in danger of being blocked by development.

As in the Santa Monica Mountains to the north, these corridors are vital to the immigration of new blood. An absence of male lions in the southern part of the Santa Ana Mountains led to a 1988 reproductive failure that resulted in a decline in lion numbers over the following three years. Without immigration of new lions, the population faces a significant risk of extinction.[20] Even *with* immigration, the amount of habitat currently protected in a contiguous block is insufficient to avoid significant extinction risk. According to Beier, "The Santa Ana Mountain Range population of mountain lions is clearly endangered due to habitat loss, loss of wildlife movement corridors, and increased mortality in vehicle collisions. Without additional protective status, the population will probably be extinct in 20 to 30 years."[21] In February of 1992, the Mountain Lion Foundation filed a petition with the U.S. Fish and Wildlife Service to list the Santa Ana Mountains population of mountain lions as an endangered species under the federal Endangered Species Act.

THE SOUTHEAST

When Spanish explorer Cabeza de Vaca sighted a cougar in Florida in the early 1500s, he was probably the first European in North America to do so. He likely never envisioned that almost 500 years later Florida would be the cats' last stronghold in the entire Southeast. Only 30 to 50 Florida panthers are thought to survive in the Everglades and surrounding wildlands,[22] and the subspecies is considered one of the rarest and most endangered mammals in the world. Named for biologist and hunter Charles B. Cory, *Felis concolor coryi* once had a range that extended from eastern Texas to Georgia, including Arkansas, Louisiana, Mississippi, Alabama, and parts of Tennessee and South Carolina.[23]

The Florida panther is generally darker and smaller than its western cousins, and its fur is short and stiff. Mature male Florida panthers weigh an average of 120 pounds and stand approximately 24 to 28 inches at the shoulder. Females are considerably smaller, with an average weight of 75 pounds and average length of about six feet. Three characteristics commonly used to identify this subspecies are a distinctive right-angle kink in the end of the tail; a whorl of hair, or "cowlick," in the middle of the back; and white flecks of hair on the head, neck, and shoulders.[24, 25] (The white flecking is due to scar tissue forming at the site of tick bites.)[25]

The panther was generally shot on sight by the first European immigrants because it was known to kill livestock and was believed to pose a danger to humans as well. By the late 1920s the lion was found only in central and south Florida, and possibly along some of the major river drainages in Louisiana.[23, 26, 27] A deer eradication program in the 1930s, undertaken to control the fever tick, drew the cats out of the protection of heavy cover in search of domestic prey and made them even more vulnerable to persecution by ranchers.[27]

Partial protection was achieved in 1950 when the pan-

ther was designated a game animal that could be hunted only during the open deer season; lions attacking livestock could still be killed if a permit was obtained. The Florida panther was given complete protection in 1958 when the Florida Game and Fresh Water Fish Commission removed it from the native game list, and finally, on March 11, 1967, when the U.S. Fish and Wildlife Service placed it on the first federal endangered species list.[25]

The remoteness and inaccessibility of this region provided panthers their greatest protection, but this changed with construction of U.S. Highway 41 (the Tamiami Trail) across Florida and through the heart of panther habitat in 1928.[25] In the 1940s, the U.S. Army Corps of Engineers began construction of a vast system of dikes and canals north and east of the region to provide flood control and to dry out the wetlands so they could be used by a rapidly growing agricultural industry. Extensive logging of the pines and cypress in the region in the late 1940s and early 1950s was followed by wildfires that swept the area. The logging and wildfires provided ideal habitat for white-tailed deer and their numbers increased until the forest canopy began closing over in the mid-1960s. It is thought that the panther population reached its highest numbers in recent times during this period.[28]

The building of State Highway 84, Alligator Alley, (1966 to 1967), sliced through the center of the region, and the construction of other access roads off this main highway greatly improved access.[25] As the vast canal system dried out much of the area, and the use of off-road vehicles became more popular, airboats and balloon-tired swamp buggies made it possible for hunters to penetrate the most remote sections of the Everglades and cypress swamps. Today, habitat disturbance is so great that there is very little wilderness left.[28]

Until a panther was treed in 1973, *Felis concolor coryi* was widely assumed to be extinct.[29] Even as late as 1977, it was unknown whether a reproducing population of panthers still existed in Florida, and if so where they might be found.[30] The discovery of survivors motivated biologists and environmentalists to take action. In 1976, the U.S. Fish and Wildlife Service formed the Florida Panther Recovery Team, made up of representatives from the Florida Game and Fresh Water Fish Commission, Department of Natural Resources, Florida Audubon Society, the National Park Service, and the Rare Feline Breeding Center. Charged with developing a plan to prevent extinction of Florida panthers in the wild, the team formulated an agenda, which was completed and approved in 1981; the research program was launched shortly thereafter. The following year the panther became Florida's official state animal.

Since 1985, a team of biologists from the Florida Game and Fresh Water Fish Commission, lead by David Maehr, has concentrated its efforts on a 2-million-acre study area in the southwest portion of the state. This area includes Fakahatchee Strand State Preserve, Big Cypress Seminole Indian Reservation, Florida Panther National Wildlife Refuge, and (unfortunately for

panthers) extensive private lands. National Park Service biologists Deborah Jansen and Sonny Bass conduct parallel studies in adjacent Big Cypress National Preserve and Everglades National Park respectively.

The panthers make their way in an amazingly flat landscape covered with a mixture of pine and hardwood forests and primeval cypress swamps, where they hunt white-tailed deer and wild hogs under cover of darkness.[22] Radio-telemetry studies show that resident male panthers have large home ranges, averaging over 300 square miles, while females have smaller ranges of about 120 square miles.[31] Unfortunately, the healthiest cats live on the private lands west and south of Lake Okeechobee, which lie to the north of the large tracts of protected public land.[32] Most of these private lands, which are now managed for low density, free-ranging cattle, provide better cover for the panthers, as well as greater concentrations of deer and hogs.[25] Another field survey indicates that the number of cats living on public lands in the southern end of their range has decreased since 1981.[33]

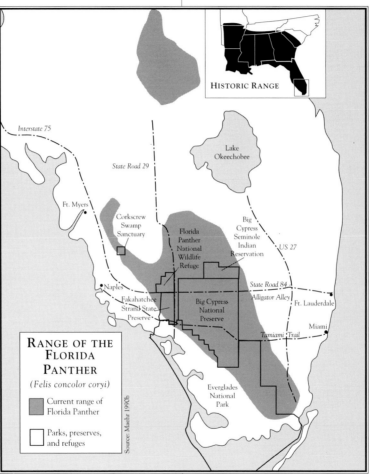

HISTORIC RANGE

Interstate 75

State Road 29

Lake Okeechobee

Ft. Myers

Corkscrew Swamp Sanctuary

Florida Panther National Wildlife Refuge

Big Cypress Seminole Indian Reservation

US 27

Naples

State Road 84

Fakahatchee Strand State Preserve

Big Cypress National Preserve

Alligator Alley

Ft. Lauderdale

Miami

Tamiami Trail

Everglades National Park

RANGE OF THE FLORIDA PANTHER
(*Felis concolor coryi*)

Current range of Florida Panther

Parks, preserves, and refuges

Source: Maehr 1990b

Ten years of study have revealed two major threats facing the Florida panther: inbreeding and habitat loss. As expected in a population so small (30 to 50 cats), signs of inbreeding are starting to show up in individuals. In addition to the kink in the tail and the "cowlick" whorl of hair, almost 90 percent of the sperm samples taken from male panthers are abnormal. Male panthers also show a high rate of cryptochidism, a condition where one testicle does not descend into the scrotum. Other suspected consequences of inbreeding may not be as easy to detect: reduced fertility, birth defects, higher mortality among newborns, slower growth, perhaps even a damaged immune system that could leave the entire panther population vulnerable to disease.[29]

Currently, the Florida panther population is too small to survive in the wild. Calculations indicate that the panther is experiencing a population decline of 6 to 10 percent a year, with a current rate of loss of genetic diversity of 3 to 7 percent per generation. This will accelerate as the population grows smaller. Therefore, extinction is possible in 25 to 40 years. In the event of a major disease sweeping through the population, extinction could be immediate. Smaller subpopulations—once found in Everglades National Park and the Raccoon Point area of Big Cypress National Preserve—are already extinct.[34] The last two female panthers known to frequent Everglades National Park both died in the summer of 1991. One died of apparent kidney failure and the other was emaciated and had an infection from a puncture wound.[35]

Equally disturbing was the discovery that the female that died from kidney failure also had elevated levels of mercury in her blood. Two years earlier, mercury was strongly implicated in the death of another female panther, also in Everglades National Park. The source of the mercury is a mystery, but experts suspect the panthers are picking it up from eating raccoons. This may explain why the higher levels of mercury are being found in cats in the southern part of their range; where there are fewer deer and

hogs, the panthers are forced to kill smaller prey such as raccoons. The mercury could be coming from both natural and man-made sources and is thought to be entering the aquatic food chain, where it is transferred to mammals such as the raccoon who regularly feed on fish. Efforts are being made to identify the source of the metal;[36] in light of the fact that the reproductive success of female panthers is lower in areas where small prey is the predominant food source, the population's foothold is made even more tenuous.

Dave Maehr is more optimistic when discussing the panther. He points out that the cats in his study area are surprisingly healthy, not the malnourished, parasite-infested, disease-ridden animals so often depicted. Females also seem to be producing healthy litters and the population has low turnover. He further suggests that panthers may tolerate a greater degree of inbreeding than was previously thought.[37]

Dennis Jordan has been the Florida Panther Recovery Coordinator, a U.S. Fish and Wildlife Service position, since 1987. Jordan states that it is the opinion of most scientists involved in the panther program that enough young cats are surviving across the entire wild population to replace those that die, at least in recent years, although some smaller populations, such as in Everglades National Park, have declined.[40]

Neither Maehr nor Jordan are complacent about the cat's future. Both emphasize that while the panther's small numbers and subsequent inbreeding are important problems, solving them will make little difference if the cats have nowhere to live. As is true elsewhere, the panther population in southern Florida appears to be limited primarily by the availability of suitable habitat. Although the lion has been legally protected for more than 20 years, human encroachment on its habitat has caused a continued decline in panther numbers. It is estimated that almost 1,000 new human residents arrive in Florida every day; most settle on the west and east coasts, resulting in rampant growth that is squeezing the Everglades and Big Cypress Swamp in the middle. In Collier County alone (where a significant panther population exists), human population growth is expected to increase 46 percent between 1985 and 1995.[41] Broward and Palm Beach counties will lead the state in numbers of new residents during this same period.

To the north, on the private lands that currently support panthers, inheritance taxes are forcing the break-up of large parcels. Their subsequent conversion to intensive agriculture may eliminate the lands as suitable panther habitat in the near future. Recent winter freezes in central Florida have killed many of the citrus groves in the region, and many growers are moving their operation farther south into these private holdings because they are less susceptible to crop-killing frosts.[25]

To accommodate the increased motor vehicle traffic between the two coasts, the Florida Department of Transportation is widening the east-west Alligator Alley into Interstate 75. The freeway cuts across the northern end of Big Cypress National Preserve and will prove a formidable obstacle where panther travel corridors intersect the freeway. Between 1979 and 1991, highway collisions accounted for almost 50 percent of all panther deaths, making it the leading cause of mortality in the lion population. Most of the unfortunate cats resided adjacent to Alligator Alley and nearby Highway 29.[40]

However, the conversion of Alligator Alley to Interstate 75 is also symbolic of a major shift in Florida's attitude toward wildlife and the environment. As part of the construction, the Department of Transportation is building 36 underpasses and other special structures to allow safe passage of wildlife along a 40-mile segment of the future interstate, at a cost of $25 million. To prevent panthers and other game from attempting to cross the freeway, a 10-foot-high chain link fence, topped by 2-foot strands of barbed wire, will be constructed along the same segment of road at an additional cost of $4.5 million.[42]

The freeway modifications are only a part of an unprecedented cooperative effort on the part of an array of governmental and environmental organizations to save the panther and other Florida wildlife. The federal government has added over 80,000 acres to Big Cypress National Preserve and over 100,000 acres to Everglades National Park. In 1989, the 30,000-acre Florida Panther National Wildlife Refuge was created to protect panthers, wood storks, snail kites, bald eagles, red-cockaded woodpeckers, peregrine falcons, and eastern indigo snakes—all endangered species. The state of Florida recently legislated one of the most aggressive public land acquisition programs in the country, committing $300 million a year for ten years.[32] Further, Dennis Jordan recently announced that a Florida Panther Habitat Preservation Plan is about to be released, one which will target critical tracts of land in panther habitat for acquisition.[42]

While such ambitious land acquisition efforts are encouraging, government cannot buy the entire state, and for this reason the role of the private land owner in the successful recovery of the Florida panther is vital. In 1990, Maehr noted: "Intensive efforts to protect Florida panther (*Felis concolor coryi*) habitat on private lands are essential for this endangered animal to survive. About half of the presently known occupied panther range in south Florida occurs on private lands where agricultural and urban development are increasing rapidly. Panther conservation strategies must go beyond traditional land acquisition by government and include economic programs to preserve critical landscapes on private lands."[43]

In addition to research and habitat conservation, officials have taken other steps toward panther protection. Reduced speed zones have been put into effect along strategic segments of highways and roads that pass through panther habitat. Large informational signs signaling the entrance into the panther's range have been erected at each end of Alligator Alley. Attempts to increase food sup-

plies of deer and hogs are being made by regulating hunting in Big Cypress National Preserve and adjacent state lands. The Florida Game and Fresh Water Fish Commission has placed a limit on the use of all-terrain vehicles and restricted hunting with dogs; a court order to remove illegal hunting camps from Big Cypress National Preserve further reduced hunting pressure. The commission has also completely closed hunting for deer and wild hogs in Fakahatchee Strand, on the western edge of Big Cypress National Preserve, because of problems with illegal trespass.[25]

    Perhaps the most promising and, at the same time,

most controversial proposal for the panther is the captive breeding/reintroduction program. Officially approved January 9, 1990, this complex species-survival plan has been drawn up through the cooperative efforts of the U.S. Fish and Wildlife Service, National Park Service, Florida Game and Fresh Water Fish Commission, and Florida Department of Natural Resources. The plan calls for the removal from the wild of one to two adult panther pairs and up to six kittens annually for the following three years. The cats will be bred in captivity in hopes of establishing a population of 130 breeding animals by the year 2000 and

500 by 2010. These cats will then eventually be released into selected areas within Florida. The survival plan makes it clear that captive breeding will augment the existing capture and tracking program and is not meant to replace it.[34] Unlike the red wolf, blackfooted ferret, and California condor captive-breeding projects, which removed the entire known population from the wild, only a portion of the panther population will be identified for capture.[32] "The primary objective of the recovery plan is to establish three viable, self-sustaining populations within the panther's historic range," says Jordan, who wrote the Environmental Assessment proposing the captive breeding program. He also claims that they are even exploring the possibility of eventual releases in other states.[42]

Unfortunately, an attempt to reintroduce seven cougars captured in western Texas into Osceola National Forest, near the Florida-Georgia border, in 1988, met with failure. Things went well in the early stages of the experiment; the area seemed to have adequate cover and plentiful deer. The cougars established home ranges, killed deer and hogs regularly, and began to develop a social structure. Then the deer hunting season arrived. One cougar died of unknown causes, two more were shot, and the remaining four began to wander from the forest and had to be recaptured less than a year after the original release.[32]

Muddying the biological waters even more were the results of a genetics study that confirmed persistent rumors that at least some Florida panthers were hybrids. Stephen O'Brien (mentioned in Chapter 1) and Melody Roelke employed recently developed methods of DNA analysis to show that the population of panthers in the Everglades had at least one maternal ancestor from Central or South America. Most of the Big Cypress population showed none of the foreign genetic material, however.[45] While the new genetic material has biological benefits it raises the thorny legal question about whether the panthers are a legitimate subspecies. While some now suggest bringing in other sub-

species and introducing them into the Florida population, the U.S. Fish and Wildlife Service has taken the position that the Florida panther is an endangered isolated population and will continue to be protected under the federal Endangered Species Act.[42]

In December of 1990, the animal rights group Fund For Animals filed suit against the U.S. Fish and Wildlife Service, charging that the captive breeding program violated the National Environmental Policy Act (NEPA) and the Endangered Species Act (ESA). Their major concerns were that inadequate attention had been paid to reintroduction feasibility, panther habitat identification and preservation, the feasibility of introduction of related subspecies, and the impact of removing panthers from the population. They also requested a more thorough review of the impacts of hunting and off-road vehicle use on panther survival. A settlement was reached in early 1991 and the USFWS agreed to prepare a Supplemental Environmental Assessment addressing the issues identified by the Fund for Animals. Government officials also agreed to remove only six kittens in 1991, and no additional kittens until the supplemental document was finalized. The first six kittens were successfully captured and the Supplemental Environmental Assessment has been released. The Fund for Animals has found the supplemental assessment acceptable for now, but will be watching the program closely. Plans are now underway to capture another six kittens in 1992.[42,45]

Rescuing an endangered species is not cheap. At present, almost $1 million is being spent yearly by various state and federal agencies to recover the Florida panther.[25] The collective price tag of a captive-breeding facility, development of reproductive technology, and genetic investigations has been placed at $526,000,[34] while the modifications to Interstate 75 cost a whopping $29.5 million.[41] Are such enormous expenditures worth it? Absolutely. What is at stake is not only the future of the Florida panther, but the future of the entire wetland ecosystem of southern

Florida. There is a lesson here as well for states and provinces that still have healthy wildlife populations. Good habitat conservation planning and acquisition now is far more economical than the exhaustive recovery efforts needed later to prevent a species from slipping into extinction.

Dave Maehr puts it another way: "All it would take to save the Florida panther is [the price of] one B-1 bomber."[37] Think about it.

THE NORTHEAST

Sightings of the elusive eastern panther, long thought to be extinct in the Northeast, seem to be increasing. The regeneration of the northeastern forests, along with increasing deer numbers and the return of many other wildlife species, would seem to support the possibility of the cat's return. In October 1990, a rabbit hunter says he treed a cougar with his dog in upstate New York. Another individual claims to have recently captured a cougar on videotape near Waasis, New Brunswick.[46] (The blurry image is questioned by Canadian wildlife officials.) Park employees watched cougars stalking deer in Great Smoky Mountains National Park in 1975 and 1978, and multiple sightings of a female with kittens were made along the Blue Ridge Parkway in North Carolina in 1975 and 1977.[47] Additional cougar sightings have been reported throughout Maine and Vermont.

Experts generally recognize two subspecies of cougar in southeastern Canada and the northeastern United States: *F. c. schorgeri* (Wisconsin puma) once inhabited the upper Mississippi River Valley and Western Great Lakes region, which includes Iowa, Illinois, Kansas, Minnesota, Wisconsin, and parts of southern Manitoba and Ontario; the U.S. Fish and Wildlife Service lists the subspecies as a Category 2 animal.[48] *F. c. couguar* (eastern panther), listed as endangered under the federal Endangered Species Act (ESA), occupied southeastern Canada and the eastern United

States as far south as South Carolina and as far west as the Mississippi.[49]

The International Union for the Conservation of Nature (IUCN) lists the eastern panther as endangered, as does the Convention on the International Trade in Endangered Species (CITES). Canada does not have a federal law comparable to ESA—endangered species are generally given legal protection under provincial law.[50] Today the eastern panther is protected in Manitoba, Quebec, New Brunswick, and Nova Scotia .

Probably the greatest advocate for the existence of the eastern panther was the late Bruce Wright, director of the Northeastern Wildlife Station of the University of New Brunswick. From 1938 until his death in 1975 he methodically recorded reported sightings in the eastern panther's range, photographed suspected tracks, made plaster casts, confirmed panthers that had been killed in 1932 and 1938, and compiled the evidence into several articles and two books, *The Ghost of North America*[51] and *The Eastern Panther: A Question of Survival*.[52] Between 1900 and 1971 Wright listed 304 reported sightings in Quebec and the Maritimes.[53] He concluded that New Brunswick supported a small panther population.[52]

However, Wright's opinion is not shared by some academics and wildlife officials. "I would stake my life that there is no viable breeding population of panthers in the northeastern United States or southeastern Canada." So states Rainer Brocke, a professor at the State University of New York in Syracuse. Brocke completed a study in 1981 on the possibility of reintroducing panthers into Adirondack Park in upstate New York. He concluded that human and road densities would cause such high mortality in the panther population that reintroduction would not be feasible. He thinks most reliable sightings, which he places at about five percent, are escapees.[54]

But the sightings continue, many of them quite detailed. A New Brunswick wildlife technician, looking from

the cab of his parked truck, saw a deer bound across the road in front of his truck, pursued by a panther. The panther paused, glanced at the truck, and then in a bound cleared the road and ran into a cutover area. The technician had seen live and dead panthers in Alberta and was sure of what he saw. Two women, in July 1983, pulled their car to the side of a back road near Waldoboro, Maine, and watched a panther sunning itself in a large tamarack tree, approximately 60 yards distant. The women watched the cat for a full hour, until it stretched, raked its claws on the tree's trunk and sauntered off into the woods. Maine game wardens and biologists descended on the area, but found only claw marks, a handful of hairs; and two muddy four-inch-wide cat tracks.[55] In February 1991, a couple from Conway, Massachusetts, watched a panther move along the edge of a meadow while they were burning brush.[46]

Canadian biologists provided further fuel for the panther debate when they identified a resident population of panthers in the province of Manitoba in the early 1970s. The cats not only appeared to belong to the eastern subspecies but seemed to be spreading into Minnesota and Michigan.[56,57] In December 1991, Minnesota conservation officers tranquilized and captured a 100-pound, female cougar that had climbed a 30-foot tree in the residential neighborhood of Worthington in the southern part of the state.[58]

Ted Reed has picked up where Bruce Wright left off. A retired businessman and wildlife amateur, Reed is founder of Friends of the Eastern Panther, a nonprofit organization dedicated to the recovery and protection of panthers. While driving through Nova Scotia in 1974, a panther leaped across the road in front of Reed's car, an experience that made him an instant believer. He was incredulous when told that the cat was extinct. After reviewing the record of panther sightings and examining Wright's research, Reed became convinced that many of the animals sighted in southeastern Canada and New England were members of a small resident panther population that had

survived in the interior wildlands of New Brunswick. Frustrated by the reticence of wildlife agencies to conduct an investigation, Reed founded Friends of the Eastern Panther in 1989 and enlisted the help of Susan Morse and Canadian biologist Robert Rainer. Reed explains, "We've said all along we don't have 100 percent proof. All we're saying is that the evidence is so strong that it absolutely warrants an investigation."[46]

Such an investigation was conducted, but in the southern Appalachian region, not the Northeast. In 1977, conservation groups threatened litigation against the U.S. Forest Service for timber harvesting in the Nantaleala National Forest in western North Carolina, where pumas had been reported.[47] As a result, the U.S. Forest Service and the U.S. Fish and Wildlife Service jointly sponsored a study to determine if the eastern panther survived. The study was undertaken by biologist Robert L. Downing, based at Clemson University in South Carolina. Downing's survey ran from 1978 to 1983 and covered Georgia, South Carolina, North Carolina, Tennessee, and Virginia. This region straddles the range of both the southeastern subspecies (*F. c. coryi*) and the eastern subspecies (*F. c. couguar*). He started by distributing over 600 one-page questionnaires containing diagrams and descriptions of panther tracks. He also circulated about 100 plaster casts of panther tracks to key biologists to verify their authenticity. Next he followed up on sighting reports, but rarely found these reliable. After five years of searching, he failed to come up with a reliable track, scrape, or scat (feces). "I never found anything," said Downing, "but it sure is hard to believe everyone who saw one was wrong."[47,59]

In a proposed recovery plan that he wrote for the eastern panther, Downing noted that the first priority of such a plan must be the location and delineation of panther populations. "Finding cougars is a top priority so that they can be given the protection and habitat they need. Conversely, obtaining information needed to say with confidence that they are not present ranks a close second. Both require the same action, a coordinated systematic, scientific search. Other priorities cannot be contemplated seriously until a population of *F. c. couguar* has been found."[60]

"The official stance of the U.S. Fish and Wildlife Service on the eastern panther is that it does not exist as a breeding species east of the Mississippi, except for the Florida panther," states Paul Nickerson, chief of the Endangered Species Division in USFWS's Northeast Region. Like Brocke, he believes most sightings are either escapees or misidentification of bobcats or dogs. "I'm still waiting for someone to provide good physical evidence, such as a track, kill, or carcass of a panther."[61]

Susan Morse wonders why wildlife officials are waiting for someone else to provide evidence of the panther's existence. "They're saying the animal doesn't exist because the evidence doesn't exist, yet they're not going out and getting the evidence, nor are they taking an aggressive stance on habitat loss. We're losing ground, literally and figuratively. That's the bottom line," claims a frustrated Morse. "We have a nongame fund here in Vermont and to date they have not invested a dime in Canada lynx or the eastern panther and that's inexcusable."[62]

How difficult can it be to find a cougar? In a 1983 issue of *New Brunswick Naturalist*, writer Gerry Parker gives an example: "On a 530-acre wilderness park at the end of a peninsula within the city of Seattle, a cougar was sighted in August 1981. The park was closed and for one full day three cat hounds combed the area to no avail. The following day the cougar was seen by police sunning itself on the main road so 6 more cat hounds were brought in. After another full day, no trace of the cougar could be found. The hounds never indicated a cougar was, or had been, in the area. It was seen again the following day along with a track and scat, the first tangible evidence of its presence in three days of hunting. The six dogs were released again in the immediate area and after 9 hours a young male cougar was

treed, tranquilized and removed from the park. This last hunt involved several Game Department people, half a dozen park employees, several Navy security personnel and numerous news people."

While panthers themselves are hard to find, biologists claim that sign they leave behind—tracks, scrapes, scat—should be fairly common in areas the cats frequent, especially females with kittens, a situation which concentrates their movements in a relatively small area. Morse, herself an experienced tracker, counters that very few biologists in the Northwest have ever seen a cougar track or scrape. She also points out that the Florida panther was thought to be extinct until someone made a concerted effort to find one. "I was a kid when sightings of coyotes in New England began to be reported," says Ted Reed. "No one believed it. All the biologists laughed and so did the newspapers. It was true. Now coyotes are everywhere."[46,62]

The position of the Canadian government on the eastern panther situation is more encouraging. According to Bruce Johnson, a wildlife biologist with the Canadian Wildlife Service's Atlantic Region, there have been 163 panther sightings in New Brunswick and 266 in Nova Scotia since 1977. There are also widespread reports from the province of Ontario. In 1985, a panther was struck and killed by a motor vehicle in Nova Scotia, though Johnson believes it was an escaped cat.[50] In 1988 the Council of Canadian Wildlife Ministers (comprised of all the provincial ministers responsible for wildlife matters) established a national strategy for the recovery of endangered species and an organization to apply it. This organization is called RENEW (an acronym for Recovery of Nationally Endangered Wildlife) and is supported by the federal, provincial, and territorial governments. Under RENEW's auspices, a number of species are receiving financial and technical assistance. Each species has a "recovery team," which is responsible for formulating recovery plans. Johnson chairs the recovery team recently formed for the eastern panther, and Susan Morse has been invited to join the team.[63]

Morse was reluctant at first to believe the eastern panther existed, but after working with lion experts throughout the West and watching the regeneration of the northeastern forests and deer herds, she is now convinced. She explains: "If a remnant population of panthers survived the devastation of the forests and deer herds, they were probably deep in the recesses of Nova Scotia or New Brunswick. It's conceivable there is a building population of panthers dining on the deer population that is growing in response to this recovering plant growth that historically did not exist. We have deer numbers way up into Canada that didn't used to exist."[62]

In an attempt to break the bureaucratic logjam, Friends of the Eastern Panther and the Mountain Lion Foundation cosponsored a two-week panther survey in New Brunswick in March 1992. Tracking specialists Jay Tischendorf and Susan Morse were on the survey team. The search concentrated on southern New Brunswick, especially the area in and around Fundy National Park. This region, particularly near the coast, is characterized by some of the most rugged topography in the province. Deep ravines and dense forest, and the national park itself, have prevented excessive development, although logging has occurred west of the park. Wright believed the area to be the breeding area of the eastern panther,[52] and the survey team looked for panther signs in and around deer "yards"—south- and southwest-facing coniferous forest stands that white-tailed deer herds use as shelter from the bitter cold northeastern winters. Ideal yards allow deer to make and utilize their own paths and move freely to and from the sheltered conifer stands to edge areas, where they feed.[62] Unfortunately, the survey turned up no signs of panthers.

A familiar threat adds a special urgency to the panther survey team's search. The Fundy Trail is a proposed highway that will be built from St. Martins, New Brunswick, and travel seven miles along a totally undeveloped portion of the Bay of Fundy coast, and then turn inland and cut 20 miles through rugged, unsettled terrain, eventually entering Fundy National Park from the west. The provincial government of New Brunswick, Fundy Trail Development Association, and various chambers of commerce support the building of the road, while a group called the Fundy Wilderness Coalition opposes it. In place of the highway, the coalition proposes a hiking trail that would skirt the coast from St. Martins to Fundy National Park, offering a coastal wilderness experience unequalled in the northeast.[46] This divisive issue will likely have a major impact on the future of the eastern panther.

ENDANGERED AND WHAT IT MEANS

Some feel concern for the cougar's future is premature because neither Canadian nor United States wildlife officials have declared the big cat an endangered species. But to infer from this that there is no cause for concern is to assume that endangered status is a type of biological tripwire that indicates when we should worry. This assumption overestimates our ability to make such a designation with accuracy and to implement protective measures. Sadly, the currently popular aphorism—"endangered means there is still time,"—is frequently untrue. In the case of large predators, past evidence indicates such a designation is simply a prelude to the oblivion of extinction.

The U.S. Endangered Species Act of 1973 was designed to identify and protect plant and animal species whose number and habitat have become sufficiently depleted to critically threaten their survival. The act as amended specifically affords protection to three biological categories: species, subspecies, and populations.[64] This is why eastern subspecies of *Felis concolor*, the eastern panther and Florida panther, are listed as endangered, while most subspecies in the West are not. Under the act, once federal authorities

have evidence that a species is endangered (facing extinction in the foreseeable future in all or a major part of its
habitat) or threatened (likely to become endangered in
the foreseeable future), they are required to adopt a plan
for recovery. Only 60 percent of the 618 endangered and
threatened plant and animal species in the United States
are covered by a recovery plan. Such recovery programs
are enormously expensive, labor intensive (as shown by the
Florida panther), and often of questionable effectiveness:
In the almost 20 years since the act was adopted, only six
of the 618 animals and plants on the endangered species
list in North America have been pronounced recovered:
the American alligator, the brown pelican in several east-

ern states, three birds on Paulau (a U.S. territory in the
Pacific), and the Rydberg milkvetch.[49]

On the negative side of the biological ledger, seven
listed domestic species have been declared extinct since
1973. Currently there is a backlog of more than 600 imper-
iled species awaiting listing and federal protection. These
species are classified as Category 1, meaning substantial information exists to warrant immediate species protection.
Incredibly, another 3,500 species languish on the Category
2 list, which identifies species that are suspected of being
threatened or endangered but on which there is insufficient
information for listing. Some will likely become extinct
before an examination of their status is even attempted.[65]

STATUS OF SELECTED SUBSPECIES OF COUGAR

COMMON NAME	SCIENTIFIC NAME	HISTORIC RANGE	US FISH AND WILDLIFE SERVICE LISTING (DATE LISTED)	IUCN[1] MAMMAL RED DATA BOOK LISTING 1982	CITES[2] LISTING (DATE LISTED)
Eastern cougar or Eastern panther	F. c. couguar	Eastern North America	Endangered (1973)	Endangered	Appendix I[4] 1975
Florida panther	F. c. coryi	USA (LA & AR east to SC & FL)	Endangered (1967)	Endangered	Appendix I[4] 1975
Costa Rican puma	F. c. costaricensis	Nicaragua, Panama, Costa Rica	Endangered (1976)	—	Appendix I[4] 1975
Yuma puma	F. c. browni	AZ, CA, Mexico	Category 2[3]	—	—
Wisconsin puma	F. c. schorgeri	IA, IL, KS, MN, MD, WI, Canada	Category 2[3]	—	—

[1] International Union for the Conservation of Nature and Natural Resources. [2] Convention on International Trade in Endangered Species of Wild Fauna and Flora. [3] Category 2 comprises species or subspecies for which information now in possession of the U.S Fish and Wildlife Service indicates that proposing to list is probably appropriate, but for which conclusive data on biological vulerability and threat are not currently available to support proposed rules. [4] Appendix I = "Indeterminate" - species or subspecies known to be endangered, vulnerable, or rare but where there is not enough information to say which of the three categories is best.
Sources: Thornback and Jenkins 1982; McMahan 1982; U.S. Department of the Interior 1989; U.S. Fish and Wildlife Service 1991.

While the U.S. Fish and Wildlife Service does not consider *Felis concolor* an endangered species, they do list three subspecies as endangered (eastern panther, Florida panther, Costa Rica puma), and two subspecies as Category 2 animals (Wisconsin puma and Yuma puma). Two cougar populations in and around developed portions of southern California are fast losing critical habitat and are in danger of extirpation, and the status of cougars in Mexico, Central, and South America is unknown. International wildlife organizations publish similar listings. The International Union for the Conservation of Nature (IUCN) lists the eastern panther and Florida panther as endangered,[66] while the Convention on the International Trade in Endangered Species (CITES), classifies the eastern panther, Florida panther, and Costa Rican puma under Appendix I. This means the subspecies are known to be endangered, vulnerable, or rare, but not enough information exists to say which of the categories is best,[67] (see table, page 102). As a result, though the cougar may not be officially considered endangered or threatened as a species, some subspecies and populations are definitely in trouble.

The cougar offers an opportunity to set a new precedent in the management of large predators. The grizzly bear, wolf, and jaguar were almost driven out of existence, but the cougar endures. In some cases it survives *in spite of* management efforts, not *because of* them. The cougar is not an endangered species, and we can take steps now to insure that it never is.

CHAPTER 6. THE COUGAR IS ENDANGERED: TRUE OR FALSE? (NOTES)

1. Anderson, A.E. 1983. *A critical review of literature on puma (Felis concolor).* Colorado Division of Wildlife. Special Report Number 54.

2. Nowak, R.M. 1976. *The cougar in the United States and Canada.* New York Zoological Society and U.S. Fish and Wildlife Service Office of Endangered Species, Washington, D.C.

3. Hebert, D. 1989. The status and management of cougar in British Columbia 1988. Pages 11–14 in R.H. Smith, ed. *Proceedings of the third mountain lion workshop*, Prescott, Arizona.

4. Mansfield, T.M. and R.A. Weaver. 1989. The status of mountain lions in California. Pages 15–18 in R.H. Smith, ed. *Proceedings of the third mountain lion workshop*, Prescott, Arizona.

5. Anderson, A.E. and R.J. Tully. 1989. Status of the mountain lion in Colorado. Pages 19–23 in R.H. Smith, ed. *Proceedings of the third mountain lion workshop*, Prescott, Arizona.

6. Stiver, S.J. 1989. Status of mountain lions in Nevada. Pages 26–29 in R.H. Smith, ed. *Proceedings of the third mountain lion workshop*, Prescott, Arizona.

7. Russ, W.B. 1989. Status of the mountain lion in Texas. Pages 30–31 in R.H. Smith, ed. *Proceedings of the third mountain lion workshop*, Prescott, Arizona.

8. Shorma, G. 1989. Status of the mountain lion in Wyoming. Pages 38–39 in R.H. Smith, ed. *Proceedings of the third mountain lion workshop*, Prescott, Arizona.

9. Smith, R.H., ed. 1989. *Proceedings of the third mountain lion workshop.* Prescott, Arizona.

10. Beier, P. 1991. Cougar attacks on humans in the United States and Canada. *Wildlife Society Bulletin* 19:403–412.

11. Loftis, R.L. 1991. Protection for mountain lions sought: Sierra Club wants killings limited. *The Dallas Morning News*, 12 December 1991.

12. Sansome, A. 1992. Executive Director, Texas Parks and Wildlife Department. Austin, Texas. (Personal communication)

13. Gabbert, A. and F.R. Henderson. 1990. *Puma in Kansas.* Cooperative Extension Service. Kansas State University. Manhattan, Kansas. July 1990.

14. Benzon, T. 1991. Game Specialist, South Dakota Game, Fish and Parks Department, Rapid City, South Dakota. (Personal communication)

15. Mountain lion felled by hunter. 1991. *Denver Post*, 17 November 1991.

16. Duke, R., R. Klinger, R. Hopkins, and M. Kutilek. 1987. *Yuma puma (Felis concolor browni)*. Feasibility Report Population Status Survey. 22 September 1987. Harvey and Stanley Associates, Inc. Alviso, California. Completed for the Bureau of Reclamation.

17. Johnson, T.B. 1990. Yuma puma. *Wildlife Views*. Arizona Game and Fish Department. Phoenix, Arizona. August.

18. Edelman, P. 1990. *Critical wildlife corridor/habitat linkage areas between the Santa Susanna Mountains, the Simi Hills and the Santa Monica Mountains*. Prepared for the Nature Conservancy. The Santa Monica Mountains Conservancy. Malibu, California.

19. Manion. S. 1992. Biogeographer. Topanga–Las Virgenes Resource Conservation District. Topanga, California. (Personal communication)

20. Beier, P. 1992a. Determining minimum habitat areas and habitat corridors for cougars. *Conservation Biology* 6:In Press.

21. Beier, P. 1992b. Project Leader, Orange County Cooperative Mountain Lion Study, Department of Forestry and Resource Management, University of California, Berkeley. (Personal communication)

22. Maehr, D.S. 1990b. Tracking Florida's panthers. *Defenders*. September/October:10-15.

23. Young, S.P. and E.A. Goldman. 1946. *The puma: Mysterious American cat*. American Wildlife Institute, Washington, D.C.

24. U.S. Fish and Wildlife Service. 1987. *Florida panther recovery plan*. Technical Subcommittee of the Florida Panther Interagency Committee. June 1987.

25. Belden, R.C. 1989. The Florida panther. Pages 515–532 *in Audubon wildlife report 1988/89*. National Audubon Society. New York, New York.

26. Lowery, G.H. Jr. 1936. A preliminary report on the distribution of the mammals of Louisiana. *Proceedings of the Louisiana Academy of Sciences* 3:11–39. (Cited from Belden 1989.)

27. Tinsley, J.B. 1970. *The Florida panther*. Great Outdoors Publishing. St. Petersburg, Florida. (Cited from Belden 1989.)

28. Belden, R.C. 1986. Florida panther investigation–a progress report. Pages 159–172 *in* S.D. Miller and D.D. Everett, eds. *Cats of the world: Biology, conservation and management*. Proceedings of the Second International Cat Symposium. Caesare Kleberg Wildlife Research Institute. Kingsville, Texas.

29. Fergus, C. 1991. The Florida panther verges on extinction. *Science*. 251:1178–1180.

30. Belden, R.C. 1977. If you see a panther. *Florida Wildlife* 31:31–34.

31. Maehr, D.S., E.D. Land, and J.C. Roof. 1991a. Social ecology of Florida panthers. *National Geographic Research & Exploration*. 7(4):414–431.

32. Bolgiano, C. 1991a. Concepts of cougar. *Wilderness*, (Summer):26–33.

33. Robertson, W.B., Jr., O.L. Bass Jr., and R.T. McBride. 1985. *Review of existing information of the Florida panther in the Everglades National Park, Big Cypress National Preserve and Environs with suggestions for need and research*. Everglades National Park. Homestead, Florida. (Cited from Belden 1989.)

34. Seal, U.S., R.C. Lacy, and workshop participants. 1989. *Florida panther viability analysis and species survival plan*. Captive Breeding Specialist Group, Species Survival Commission, IUCN. Gainsville, Florida.

35. Bass, O.L. 1991. Wildlife Biologist, Everglades National Park Research Center, Homestead, Florida. (Personal communication)

36. Jordan, D. 1990a. Mercury contamination: Another threat to the Florida panther. *Endangered Species Technical Bulletin* 15(2). Department of the Interior, U.S. Fish and Wildlife Service, Washington, DC.

37. Maehr, D.S. 1992. Leader, Panther Research Team. Florida Game and Fresh Water Fish Commission, Naples, Florida. (Personal communication)

38. Jordan, D. 1990b. *Final environmental assessment: A proposal to issue endangered species permits to capture select Florida panthers and establish a captive population*. U.S. Fish and Wildlife Service. Gainsville, Florida.

39. Kiplinger Washington Editors. 1985. *1985 Kiplinger forecast of Florida's growth during the next ten years - by localities*. The Kiplinger Washington Editors, Inc. Washington, DC.

40. Maehr, D.S., E.D. Land, and M.E. Roelke. 1991b. Mortality patterns of panthers in southwest Florida. *Proceedings of the Annual Conference of Southeast Fish and Wildlife Agencies* 45:In press.

41. Harpster, J. 1990. Floridians fight to save panthers. *The Christian Science Monitor*, 24 April 1990.

42. Jordan, D. 1992. Florida Panther Coordinator, U.S. Fish and Wildlife Service, Gainsville, Florida. (Personal communication)

43. Maehr, D.S. 1990a. The Florida panther and private lands. *Conservation Biology* 4(2):167–170.

44. O'Brien, S.J., M.E. Roelke, N. Yuhki, K.W. Richards, W.E. Johnson, W. L. Franklin, A.E. Anderson, O.L. Bass Jr., R.C. Belden, and J.S. Martenson. 1990. Genetic introgression within the Florida panther *Felis concolor coryi. National Geographic Research* 6(4):485–494.

45. Schubert, D.J. 1991. Director of Investigations, The Fund for Animals Inc., Silver Springs, Maryland. (Personal communication)

46. Reed, T. 1991. President, Friends of the Eastern Panther. Exeter, New Hampshire. (Personal communication)

47. Downing, R.L. 1981a. The current status of the cougar in the southern Appalachian. Pages 142–151 *in Proceedings of the nongame and endangered wildlife symposium.* Athens, Georgia. August 13–14, 1981.

48. U.S. Department of the Interior/Fish and Wildlife Service. 1989. Endangered and threatened wildlife and plants; animal notice of review. *Federal Register,* January 6, 1989.

49. U.S. Fish and Wildlife Service. 1991. *Endangered and threatened wildlife and plants, 50 CFR 17.11 & 17.12, July 15, 1991.* U.S. Government Printing Office: 1991-296-520:50024. Washington D.C.

50. Johnson, B. 1991. Wildlife Biologist, Atlantic Region, Canadian Wildlife Service, Sackville, New Brunswick. (Personal communication)

51. Wright, B.S. 1959. *The ghost of North America: The story of the eastern panther.* Vantage Press, New York.

52. Wright, B.S. 1972. *The eastern panther: A question of survival.* Clark Irwin, Toronto.

53. Burnett, J.A., C.T. Dauphine Jr., S.H. McCrindle, and T. Mosquin. 1989. *On the brink: Endangered species in Canada.* Western Producer Prairie Books, Saskatoon, Saskatchewan.

54. Brocke, R.H. 1991. Associate Professor of Wildlife Ecology, State University of New York, College of Environmental Sciences and Forestry, Syracuse, New York. (Personal communication)

55. Adams, H. 1985. The shadow stalks, but does the panther? *Habitat* (August): 28–30.

56. Nero, R.W. and R.E. Wrigley. 1977. Status and habits of the cougar in Manitoba. *The Canadian Field-Naturalist* 91:28–40.

57. Wallace, J. 1986. Has the big cat come back? *Sierra* (May/June):20–21.

58. Wild cougar captured in Worthington. 1991b. *Austin Herald,* 23 December 1991.

59. Downing, R.L. 1991. Wildlife Biologist (retired). U.S. Fish and Wildlife Service, Denver Wildlife Research Center, Department of Forestry, Clemson University, Clemson, South Carolina. (Personal communication)

60. Downing, R.L. 1981b. *Eastern cougar recovery plan* (technical draft). Denver Wildlife Research Center. Department of Forestry. Clemson University. Clemson, South Carolina.

61. Nickerson, P. 1991. Chief of Endangered Species Division, Region 5, U.S. Fish and Wildlife Service, Boston, Massachusetts. (Personal communication)

62. Morse, S.C. 1991. Forest Ecologist and Wildlife Habitat Consultant. Morse and Morse Forestry. Jericho, Vermont. (Personal communication)

63. Rainer, R. 1991. Director, Friends of the Eastern Panther. Fredericton, New Brunswick. (Personal communication)

64. O'Brien, S.J. and Mayr E. 1991. Bureaucratic mischief: Recognizing endangered species and subspecies. *Science* 251:1187–1188.

65. Palmer, T. 1991. The final act? *Buzzworm: The Environmental Journal* (November/December):31–35.

66. Thornback, J. and M. Jenkins, eds. 1982. *The IUCN Mammal Red Data Book, Part 1.* IUCN, Gland, Switzerland.

67. McMahan, L.R. 1982. The international cat trade. Pages 461–488 *in* S.D. Miller and D.D. Everett (eds.). *Cats of the world: Biology, conservation and management.* Proceedings of the Second International Cat Symposium. Caesare Kleberg Wildlife Research Institute. Kingsville, Texas.

WHY COUGARS SHOULD BE PROTECTED

To DISCUSS THE "VALUE" OF A WILD animal, such as the cougar, is to set off a firestorm of conflicting perspectives. Cougar hunters, guides, ranchers, deer hunters, preservationists, and biologists: all share a different perspective based on individual experience and vested interest. A new perspective of the cougar is emerging, and the rhetoric has grown more complex and divisive. Common ground must be found, because now more than ever, the future of *Felis concolor* lies in our collective hands.

THE BIOLOGICAL PERSPECTIVE

The cougar merits our concern because it is the last large carnivore that still resides in the lower 48 states in presumably significant numbers. (The grizzly bear and wolf no longer play major roles in their ecological systems.) Carnivores are sensitive indicators of the health of an ecological community.[1] As Maurice Hornocker points out, the cougar "...has the broadest distribution of any mammal in North America, so by tracking it we can find out about the changing environment. It roams from forest to desert to coastal dunes, and, because it sits at the top of the food chain along with other large carnivores, its health is an indicator of the health of everything in the chain below it."[2] Further, in *A Conservation Strategy for Large*

Carnivores in Canada, Monte Hummel states "...it could be argued that if the top predator populations are healthy, then the system as a whole is likely in good shape. Conversely, if these animals are no longer present, then the system is impoverished and will likely undergo dramatic changes to adjust to their absence."[3]

The extinction of a large predator is likely to cause a drastic reordering and simplification of the ecosystem. Because carnivores are high in the food chain, they play an integral role in moving energy through the ecosystem, a critical process on which all living things depend. From sun to plants to deer to cougar to death and decomposition— this cycle is the life force of an ecosystem.

Due to their incremental and insidious nature, loss of species and loss of habitat frequently go unnoticed. Many species of plants and animals have passed into extinction without fanfare. Such will not be the case with the cougar. Will loss of a single species cause ecosystem collapse? No, but it does lessen our rich biological diversity, something that underlies the quality of all life. Should it be cause for concern? Definitely, because whether humans believe it or not, we're players in the same game.

In the realm of predator/prey relations, Hornocker believes the cougar is important in dampening the fluctuations in mule deer populations, as well as keeping herds on the move, scaring and chasing them into areas that are not overbrowsed.[4] Is it possible that the current irruptions in white-tailed deer populations in the Northeast are related to the absence of the panther from most of the region? Perhaps.

Renowned biologist Ian McTaggert-Cowan suggests that one way to determine the minimum critical size of a protected wildlife area is to make it big enough to accommodate the minimum viable population of its top predators.[3] "If parks, nature reserves, or wildlife areas are large enough to provide such 'room at the top,' then the rest of the components of the system—the predators' prey species, the plants upon which the prey depend, the insects which depend on the plants, the soil organisms, etc.—are also probably secure," adds Hummel. This is why the cougar, along with other large carnivores, is classified as an "umbrella" species.[3] When we protect habitat for the lion, we are also protecting the other species that live there, including the ones that nurture the lion directly and indirectly, and those that simply have similar habitat requirements.[1] Again, this has the additional benefit of preserving biological diversity.

Finally, management practices directed toward the cougar can provide valuable information for the conservation of other top carnivores. Linda Sweanor explains: "Information on refuge size, corridors, and translocation success may be applied to other large felids such as the jaguar. Additionally, the areas initially managed for the long-term survival of a lion population may one day support reintroduced populations of wolves or grizzly bears. In fact, the mountain lion can serve as a surrogate in those areas where it is presently not feasible (because of public opinion) or impossible (because of inadequate numbers of individuals available for release) to reintroduce another large carnivore. This way we leave our options open; if we do not develop sound conservation practices now, we have little hope of having secure populations of large mammalian predators in the future."[1]

BEYOND BIOLOGY

When asked to comment on the contributions of the twentieth century, poet Robert Frost said: "About half of life can't be made a science of, can't ever be. We're going to learn a great deal more about that before we're through this period. That's what we'll be known for."[5] Though subjected to the intense scrutiny of our technology, the cougar still slips our grasp. This is as it should be, for we love a mystery, and this mystery drives both the cougar biologist's research and the layperson's imagination. Barry Lopez spoke eloquently of the cougar's furtive nature: "As long as men study the lion, they will learn, but it is against a certainty that they will never understand it at all. This counts as no loss. The lion retains the two things that are perhaps most dear to any animal—dignity and mystery. And with these all life deepens."[6]

Measuring the dollar value of a lion hunting tag or

livestock losses is far easier than measuring the value of a cougar's beauty, nobility, independence, power, or grace. Yet these are the qualities most frequently cited as the source of the cat's "magic." The way they look. The way they move. The way they are. A perfect marriage of stealth and strength, with a sobering singleness of purpose. Just as the warriors in the Cougar Society of the Jemez Pueblo embraced the cat as their totem of power, modern man attempts to embrace the cougar's symbolic power. High schools, colleges, and universities claim the cougar as their mascot, while both automobiles and athletic shoes wear its name. But these are human devices, human constructions. By their nature, cats dwell only temporarily in our world, in it, but never of it.

Wilderness is the cougar's domain. Here the cats carry on the free and independent lives that humans envy so. It seems ironic that cougars personify those qualities that are the foundation of the country in which they face so much adversity. While there are few who will ever see a cougar in the wild, there are many who take a special comfort in knowing they are out there. In *Incident at Eagle Ranch*, Donald Schueler describes the elusive cat as: "...the ultimate loner, a renegade presence in the wildest canyons and the wildest mountains, the sign of everything that is remote from us, everything that we have not spoiled."[7]

Some believe our treatment of predators is a measure of our own humanity. John J. Craighead and his colleagues thought so when they paraphrased Henry David Thoreau in their monograph on grizzly bear habitat. "In wilderness is the preservation of the grizzly. If the human species cannot preserve the grizzly bear, it probably can't preserve itself; for the type of human behavior that will permit the extinction of the grizzly will also permit the extinction of mankind. The motivation is an evolved irreverence for life and life systems, so deep seated in our biological past that neither human intellect, religion nor culture has yet substantially curbed it."[8] It would be easy here to substitute mountain lion for grizzly bear.

Perhaps it is time, as Aldo Leopold suggested, that we begin to view the cougar as a member of a community to which we belong, rather than as a commodity to be exploited.[9] The shift in perspective from individual species to community is more than good wildlife management. It's less arrogant, and humans could use a little humility, certainly where other animals are concerned. "We continue... to assume without question our superiority to other species," wrote Harley Shaw.[10] "Our technology is our evidence to support this assumption. After I had been close to the lion, the same technology became a sign of weakness. Consider the beast that lives on the land, feeds itself by killing the fleetest of animals without using weapons, and survives the severest of weather without technological crutches that we see as necessities. In the niche of the lion, we are not its superior, and it deserves a certain awe."

It's probably safe to assume cougars are indifferent to our efforts. They are too busy being cougars—hunting, killing, raising their young. You may never see one, but they're out there. In "Memo to the Mountain Lion," Wallace Stegner (1981) said it best, "Once, in every corner of this continent, your passing could prickle the stillness and bring every living thing to the alert. But even then you were felt more than seen. You were an immanence, a presence, a crying in the night, pug tracks in the dust of a trail. Solitary and shy, you lived beyond, always beyond. Your comings and goings defined the boundaries of the unpeopled. If seen at all, you were only a tawny glimpse flowing toward disappearance among the trees or along the ridges and ledges of your wilderness."[11]

If the ecosystem in which the cougar dwells was untouched by humans, we could allow the cat to go about its business and let nature take its course. Such a scenario is fantasy, for humans have reshaped the natural world on an unprecedented scale. No one questions our ability to dispense death to other species, and we have done so with both arrogance and efficiency. We now face the greater challenge of nurturing life. With our manipulation of the natural environment we have assumed responsibility for the cougar's welfare. Their survival is now a moral obligation.

AFTERWORD: WHY COUGARS SHOULD BE PROTECTED (NOTES)

1. Sweanor, L.L. 1990. Mountain lion social organization in a desert environment. M.S. thesis, University of Idaho, Moscow.

2. Rozek, M. 1989. The man who saved america's lion. *Ford Times* (September): 34–39.

3. Hummel, M. 1990. *A conservation strategy for large carnivores in Canada.* World Wildlife Fund Canada, Toronto.

4. Hornocker, M.G. 1970. An analysis of mountain lion predation upon mule deer and elk in the Idaho Primative Area. *Wildlife Monographs* 21:1–39.

5. Morse, S.C. 1989. Begging the question: What is mountain lion management? Pages 3-4 *in* R.H. Smith, ed. *Proceedings of the third mountain lion workshop*, Prescott, Arizona.

6. Lopez, B. 1981. The elusive mountain lion. *GEO* (June): 98–116.

7. Schueler, D.G. 1980. *Incident at Eagle Ranch: Man and predator in the American West.* Sierra Club Books. San Francisco, California.

8. Craighead, J.J., J.S. Sumner, and G.B. Scaggs. 1982. *A definitive system for analysis of grizzly bear habitat and other wilderness resources.* Wildlife-Wildlands Institute Monograph No. 1. University of Montana Foundation, University of Montana, Missoula, Montana. (Cited from Morse 1989.)

9. Leopold, A. 1949. *A sand county almanac.* Oxford University Press, London.

10. Shaw, H.G. 1989. *Soul among lions.* Johnson Books. Boulder, Colorado.

11. Stegner, W. 1981. *Memo to the mountain lion.* Written exclusively for Operation Wildlife. Mountain Lion Foundation. Sacramento, California.

WHAT NEEDS TO BE DONE:
An Action Plan for
Cougar Management and Preservation

As a symbol of the need to protect our wildlife heritage, and as a top predator that needs many acres of land to roam and survive, the cougar is a key species in efforts to protect wildlife habitat. If we can preserve the cougar and its vast habitat, we will assure the survival of many other species as well. There is a great deal that can be done to preserve cougars as a viable species, particularly in the areas of habitat protection, research, livestock protection, management, and education. Since cougars do not respect state boundaries, federal land management jurisdictions, or private property lines, any cougar management program must take a coordinated approach at the federal, state, provincial, and local levels. The Mountain Lion Foundation offers the following action plan for cougar management and preservation.

HABITAT PROTECTION

Loss of habitat is the greatest threat facing cougars, deer, and other wildlife. Habitat acquisition, enhancement, restoration, and protection are fundamental to cougar survival, as well as to the mitigation of threats from urban, residential, and agricultural development. Since the habitat needs of cougars and deer frequently overlap, both are addressed in the recommendations that follow.

RECOMMENDATIONS FOR COUGAR HABITAT:

1. Protect large, contiguous tracts of cougar habitat as wildlife preserves. These must be large enough to support healthy cougar populations.

2. Provide funding to acquire habitat and to enhance and restore habitat, including special appropriations, federal funds, and bond acts.

3. Prevent construction of barriers—roads, canals, reservoirs, croplands, or residential developments—that separate cougar populations from portions of their habitat. In those areas where cougar habitat is more fragmented, place land acquisition emphasis on habitat corridors.

4. In areas where there is a decreasing prey base, promote the increase of ungulate numbers as part of an overall biodiversity protection program.

5. Develop incentives to protect private land from development, including acquisitions, land swaps, transfer of development rights, agreements, and easements. Establishing conservation easements and cooperative wildlife protection projects on private wildlands saves tax dollars and can be innovative state/private cooperative ventures. There are many creative programs that provide incentives to land managers for voluntary habitat protection efforts.

6. Restore degraded habitats, and, where appropriate, create new habitat. For example, many eastern states now have large tracts of land no longer suitable for farming that may be able to support cougar populations.

RECOMMENDATIONS FOR DEER HABITAT:
1.   Protect large tracts of land as wildlife preserves.
2.   Support legislation that restricts the development of critical areas.
3.   Restrict development in deer migration corridors and in critical winter, summer, and fawning ranges. Prevent barriers—roads, canals, or fences—from inhibiting migration and separating deer from portions of their habitat.
4.   Provide incentives for private owners to keep the habitat they own intact, especially riparian habitat.
5.   Reduce livestock grazing allotments, where appropriate, and reduce the number of livestock allowed on each allotment. A balance must be maintained to encourage good grazing practices that benefit both wildlife and ranch owners.

RESEARCH

Comprehensive and current research, based on proven scientific methods, is the foundation of good cougar management. Unfortunately, the cougar is hard to study. Obtaining the most basic field data on cougar populations can involve enormous investments in time, money, and effort. But the more we learn about this American lion, the better we can address the problems of the many other species that share the cat's habitat.

1.   Funding and manpower must be increased to more comprehensively research the cougar's complex biology, ecology, and behavior. Such studies often need to be conducted for periods of at least five years.
2.   Research methods need to be standardized so that wildlife biologists in different states and Canadian provinces can easily exchange information.
3.   Reliable methods need to be developed to provide better census figures and age statistics on cougars.
4.   Habitat studies need to be conducted to identify preferred habitat criteria and minimum-habitat-size criteria. Other research should focus on predator/prey relations and livestock protection, as well as the impacts of hunting, human encroachment, fire, and drought on cougar populations.

LIVESTOCK PROTECTION

It is clear, based on available evidence, that the killing of livestock by cougars affects a minority of stockmen. Traditional control programs have proven both costly and ineffective. There is growing sentiment that occasional losses of livestock to cougars, at least on public land, must become accepted as part of the price of doing business. A variety of nonlethal predator control methods now available should replace past depredation reduction practices.

RECOMMENDATIONS:

1.   Ranchers and farmers should be encouraged to use nonlethal control methods to reduce livestock losses. These can include altering husbandry practices, using taste-aversion methods, installing electric fencing, or using various breeds of guard dogs. Better research is needed on the most effective measures.

2.   Livestock protection regulations need to be strengthened and more strictly enforced. Greater effort must be made to verify reported depredations. This is particularly important in programs that reimburse stockmen for losses.

3.   "Preventative" predator control practices, which involve general extermination of supposed pests through trapping, poisons, and snares, should be outlawed. Laws already exist in every western state that allow the taking of cougars that threaten people or property.

4.   The U.S. Department of Agriculture's Animal Damage Control (ADC) program should be immediately disbanded. Its continued operation cannot be biologically, morally, or financially justified.

5.   In the future, all cougars killed after attacking livestock should receive a careful postmortem examination, and the results should be filed so as to make them accessible.

MANAGEMENT

Wildlife management is generally the province of the state, and state wildlife agencies are chiefly sportsmens' organizations dedicated to providing game and fish for sport and consumption; hunting and fishing licenses are the primary source of funding. As demographics change and the quality of our wildlife and fisheries declines, wildlife administrators are being asked to shoulder a broader environmental mandate. Greater attention must be paid to "nongame" management, habitat acquisition, and environmental protection and mitigation. Wildlife professionals are also being urged to shift emphasis from managing species to managing whole biological communities. It is in this management shift that the cougar could prove to be a solution rather than a problem, for protecting cougars and their habitat helps to preserve many other wildlife and plant species.

RECOMMENDATIONS:

1.   In states that allow cougar hunting, limits should be set on the number of females harvested so as to maintain populations. Some states already have a regulation, or protect females entirely.

2. State wildlife agencies need more stable and reliable sources of funding. A larger portion of their budget needs to come from the state's general fund or other stable sources of revenue, so the agency is not dependent only on hunting and fishing license fees.

3. State wildlife agencies need additional funding to increase staff and time spent in such areas as law enforcement, habitat acquisition, nature education, and environmental protection and mitigation. Additional funding sources should be explored, such as environmental license plate fees, tax-form checkoffs, special taxes on activities that harm wildlife habitat, or charging fees to enter state wildlife refuges.

4. Those who are selected to sit on state wildlife commissions and direct fish and wildlife programs should be experienced in governmental affairs and wildlife issues, as well as representative of a variety of backgrounds and interests. This will expand the representation of the public on the commission and in day-to-day management decisions.

5. The penalties for illegally killing a cougar should be increased. Wildlife managers need to more closely monitor and quantify the impact of poaching on local cougar populations. Judges and lawyers need to be educated as to the seriousness of wildlife violations, with emphasis on the enormous toll poaching takes on our wildlife heritage each year, estimated conservatively at $200 million in the United States alone.

EDUCATION

Much of what we know about cougars has only been revealed in the last two decades. This information tends to be restricted to a small circle of research biologists who publish their findings in professional journals with limited circulations. As a result, a surprising number of myths about cougars persist, even among wildlife managers. A concerted effort must be made to enlighten children, teachers, ranchers, farmers, hunters, conservationists, and wildlife professionals as to the true nature of this remarkable cat.

RECOMMENDATIONS:

1. An educational curriculum needs to be developed for teachers to present in the classroom relating the importance of the cougar as a predator and facts about the cat's biology, ecology, and behavior. (The Mountain Lion Foundation is currently developing such a project.)

2. Rangers at federal, state, and county parks should develop and present interpretive programs about cougars for the visiting public. Informational literature should also be written and made available at visitor centers and campgrounds.

3. State wildlife agencies should develop informational literature about cougars and make in available to hunters, ranchers, and people who live in cougar country. (The Colorado Division of Wildlife currently distributes a brochure titled "The Facts About Mountain Lions.")

· A P P E N D I X   B ·

WHAT YOU CAN DO TO PROTECT COUGARS

1. Learn all you can about cougars. You have taken the first step by reading *Cougar: The American Lion*. For further information consult the list of references at the back of this book. To learn more about cougars in your own state or province contact your wildlife or game department.

2. If cougars live in your state or province, urge your legislators and wildlife/game department administrators to stop development in the cats' habitat.

3. If cougars live in your state or province, urge your legislators and wildlife/game department administrators to support funding for purchase and enhancement of critical habitat for cougars, deer, and other wildlife, and assure, through continued efforts, that funds are indeed obligated and spent in this manner.

4. If cougars live in your state or province, urge your legislators and wildlife/game department administrators to fund additional research and to base cougar management on current and sound biological information.

5. If cougar hunting is allowed in your state or province, urge that it be stopped, or at least that limits be set on the number of females killed, so that healthy populations are maintained.

6. If general depredation hunting or trapping (extermination of cougars as supposed pests) still exists, urge that it be outlawed immediately.

7. If you own livestock in cougar country, consider protecting them from cougars through husbandry methods rather than ill-advised predator-killing programs. Contact the Mountain Lion Foundation for further information.

8. Support the Mountain Lion Foundation, a private, nonprofit, research, and education organization dedicated to the protection of cougars. Support other nonprofit wildlife organizations. (Mountain Lion Foundation, P.O. Box 1896, Sacramento, CA 95812, (916) 422-2666.)

9. "Adopt" a mountain lion through the Mountain Lion Foundation's Adopt-a-Lion program. This symbolic adoption provides important financial support to the foundation's many educational and conservation programs.

10. Learn all you can about your state/provincial wildlife or game department, the U.S. Fish and Wildlife Service, and/or the Canadian Wildlife Service. Subscribe to their newsletters, request additional literature and stay informed about issues concerning wildlife and wildlife habitat.

· A P P E N D I X   C ·

THE MOUNTAIN LION FOUNDATION

THE MOUNTAIN LION FOUNDATION is a non-profit conservation and education organization dedicated to increasing understanding of and protection for mountain lions and other wildlife and their habitat around the country, with special emphasis on California.

1.   The Mountain Lion Foundation was instrumental in the passage of the California Wildlife Protection Act of 1990 (Proposition 117). This landmark legislation permanently bans the sport hunting of cougars in California, restricts depredation killing of cougars, and sets aside $30 million annually for the next 30 years for the acquisition of critical habitat for deer and mountain lions, endangered species, riparian and wetland habitats, and landscape linkages.

2.   The Mountain Lion Foundation opposes the sport hunting of mountain lions on the grounds that it is biologically and morally unjustified. Sport hunting of mountain lions is neither a legitimate wildlife management technique nor a morally justified recreational activity.

3.   The Mountain Lion Foundation believes the most critical threat facing cougars, deer, and other wildlife is loss of habitat, and that habitat acquisition, enhancement, restoration, and protection must be priorities in any cougar management program.

4.   The Mountain Lion Foundation believes there is a critical need for expanded research of the cougar's biology, ecology, and behavior. As a predator that sits high in the food chain and has a wide distribution, the cougar is a keen indicator of the environmental health of the variety of habitats in which it lives. Increased knowledge of the cougar can also benefit the other wildlife and plants in its habitat.

5.   The Mountain Lion Foundation is opposed to general depredation programs that arbitrarily destroy cougars as pests, and believes prevention of depredation through better husbandry practices is the best approach. Specific depredation can be effectively addressed through nonlethal means.

6.   The Mountain Lion Foundation believes that while the U.S. Fish and Wildlife Service does not recognize any western subspecies of *Felis concolor* as endangered or threatened, the status of the species as a whole is very much in question. While some populations seem healthy, three subspecies are listed as endangered, two other subspecies are candidates for listing, two cougar populations in southern California are on the verge of extirpation (becoming extinct in a localized area), and the status of the cat in Mexico, Central and South America is unknown.

7.   The Mountain Lion Foundation is currently developing a clearinghouse of literature on cougars. This reference

library will contain technical papers, general articles, books, state cougar management reports, lists of experts, and comprehensive bibliographies. The Mountain Lion Foundation is pleased to make this information available to wildlife professionals, students, the media, and the general public.

8.   The Mountain Lion Foundation conducts active conservation programs to protect mountain lions, acquire and protect wildlife habitat, prevent poaching, rebuild government wildlife agencies to reflect broader environmental concerns, introduce extirpated wildlife to suitable habitat and preserve our nation's rich wildlife heritage. (Mountain Lion Foundation, P.O. Box 1896, Sacramento, CA 95812, (916) 442-2666.)

9.   The Mountain Lion Foundation is currently developing educational curricula and informational literature about cougars that emphasizes their importance as predators and relates essential facts about their biology, ecology, and behavior.

·BIBLIOGRAPHY·

Ackerman, B.B. 1982. Cougar predation and ecological energetics in southern Utah. M.S. thesis, Utah State University, Logan.

———, F.G. Lindzey, and T.P. Hemker. 1984. Cougar food habits in south ern Utah. *Journal of Wildlife Management* 48:147–155.

Acuff, D.S. 1988. Perceptions of the mountain lion, 1825–1986, with emphasis on *Felis concolor californica*. M.A. thesis, University of California, Davis.

Adams, H. 1985. The shadow stalks, but does the panther? *Habitat* (*August*): 28–30.

Akeman, T. 1991a. Rancher tells why big cats were killed. *The Monterey Herald*, 26 April 1991.

———. 1991b. Rancher gets jail, fine in big-cat case. *The Monterey Herald*, 17 August 1991.

Alexander, H.B. 1916. *The mythology of all races: North America*. Cambridge: Cambridge University Press. (Cited from Acuff 1988.)

Anderson, A.E. 1983. *A critical review of literature on puma (Felis concolor)*. Colorado Division of Wildlife. Special Report Number 54.

———, and R.J. Tully. 1989. Status of the mountain lion in Colorado. Pages 19–23 in R.H. Smith, ed. *Proceedings of the third mountain lion workshop*, Prescott, Arizona.

Armentrout, D. 1984. Toward a national predator policy. Paper presented at National Audubon Society, Western Regional Conference, Asilomar, California.

Ashman, D., G.C. Christensen, M.L. Hess, G.K. Tsukamoto, and M.S. Wickersham. 1983. *The mountain lion in Nevada*. Nevada Department of Wildlife, Reno.

———. 1977. *Mountain lion investigations*. Job Performance Report, Project W-48-8. Nevada Dept. Wildlife, Reno, Nevada. (Cited from Dixon 1982.)

Austin, P. 1991. Who owns the wilderness in the northern forest? *The Sacramento Bee*, 10 July 1991.

Barnes, C.T. 1960. *The cougar or mountain lion*. Salt Lake City. Ralton Co.

Barnhurst, D.E. 1986. Vulnerability of cougars to hunting. M.S. thesis, Utah State University, Logan.

Bass, O.L., and D.S. Maehr. 1991. Do recent deaths in Everglades National Park suggest an ephemeral population? *National Geographic Research & Exploration* 7(4):427.

Beier, P. 1991. Cougar attacks on humans in the United States and Canada. *Wildlife Society Bulletin* 19:403–412.

———. 1992. Determining minimum habitat areas and habitat corridors for cougars. *Conservation Biology* 6:In Press.

Belden, R.C. 1977. If you see a panther. *Florida Wildlife* 31:31–34.

———. 1986. Florida panther investigation—a progress report. Pages 159–172 *in* S.D. Miller and D.D. Everett, eds. *Cats of the world: Biology, conservation and management.* Proceedings of the Second International Cat Symposium. Caesare Kleberg Wildlife Research Institute. Kingsville, Texas.

———. 1989. The Florida panther. Pages 515–532 *in Audubon wildlife report 1988/89.* National Audubon Society. New York.

Bensimhon, D., and M. Brophy. 1992. Man-killers. *Men's Health* (April):79.

Bogue, G., and M. Ferrari. 1974. The predatory "training" of captive reared pumas. Pages 36–45 *in* R.L. Eaton, ed. *The world's cats, vol. 3(1): Contributions to status, management and conservation.* Carnivore Research Institute, University of Washington, Seattle. (Cited from Dixon (1982.)

Bolgiano, C. 1991a. Concepts of cougar. *Wilderness* (Summer):26–33.

———. 1991b. Of panthers and prejudice. *Buzzworm: The Environmental Journal* (May/June):47–51.

Bowns, J.E. 1985. Predation-depredation. Pages 204–215 *in* J. Roberson and F.G. Lindzey, eds. *Proceedings of the second mountain lion workshop,* Salt Lake City, Utah.

Brocke, R.H. 1981. *Reintroduction of the cougar* Felis concolor *in Adirondack Park: A problem analysis and recommendations.* Federal Aid Project E-1-3. U.S. Fish and Wildlife Service and New York State Department of Environmental Conservation.

Burnett, J.A., C.T. Dauphine Jr., S.H. McCrindle, and T. Mosquin. 1989. *On the brink: Endangered species in Canada.* Western Producer Prairie Books, Saskatoon, Saskatchewan.

California Department of Fish and Game. 1988. *Mountain lion depredation summary statewide.* Sacramento.

California Senate Office of Research Issue Brief. 1987. *The crime of poaching. August.*

Conklin, W.A. 1884. *The mammals of the Adirondack Region, northeastern New York.* L.S. Foster Press, New York, (Cited from Dixon 1982.)

Connolly, G.E. 1978. Predators and predator control. Pages 369–394 *in* J.L. Schmidt and D.L. Gilbert, eds. *Big game of North America: Ecology and management.* Wildlife Management Institute. Stackpole Books.

Craighead, J.J., J.S. Sumner, and G.B. Scaggs. 1982. *A definitive system for analysis of grizzly bear habitat and other wilderness resources.* Wildlife-Wildlands Institute Monograph No. 1. University of Montana Foundation, University of Montana, Missoula, Montana. (Cited from Morse 1989.)

Currier, M.J.P. 1983. *Felis concolor.* Mammalian Species No. 200, pp. 1–7. American Society of Mammalogists.

Cunningham, E.B. 1971. A cougar kills an elk. *Canadian Field Naturalist* 85:253–254. (Cited from Dixon 1982.)

Dagget, D. 1988. Dishonorable discharges. *New Times* (August): 18–23.

Danvir, R.E., and F.G. Lindzey. 1981. Feeding behavior of a captive cougar on mule deer. *Encyclia* 58:50–56. Utah Academy of Sciences.

Dassman, R.F. 1981. *Wildlife biology,* 2nd edition. John Wiley and Sons, New York.

Dixon, K.R. 1967. *Mountain lion predation on big game and live stock in Colorado.* Job Completion Rep. Proj. W-38-R-21, Colorado Game, Fish, Parks Dept., Fort Collins, Colo. (Cited from Dixon 1982.)

———. 1982. Mountain lion. Pages 711–727 *in* J.A. Chapman and G.A. Feldhamer, eds. *Wild mammals of North America.* John Hopkins University Press. Baltimore.

Downing, R.L. 1981a. The current status of the cougar in the southern Appalachian. Pages 142–151 in *Proceedings of the nongame and endangered wildlife symposium*. Athens, Georgia. August 13–14, 1981.

———. 1981b. *Eastern cougar recovery plan* (technical draft). Denver Wildlife Research Center. Department of Forestry. Clemson University. Clemson, South Carolina. 14pp.

Duke, R., R. Klinger, R. Hopkins, and M. Kutilek. 1987. *Yuma puma (Felis concolor browni)*. Feasibility Report Population Status Survey. September 22, 1987. Harvey and Stanley Associates, Inc. Alviso, California. Completed for the Bureau of Reclamation.

Eaton, R.L. 1976. Why some felids copulate so much. *World's cats* 3:73–94. (Cited from Anderson 1983.)

———, and K.A. Velander. 1977. Reproduction in the puma: Biology, behavior and ontogeny. Pages 45–70 in R.L. Eaton, ed. *The world's cats, vol. 3(3): Contributions to breeding biology, behavior and husbandry*. Carnivore Research Institute, University of Washington, Seattle.

Eaton, Eric. 1987. Man and the cougar: Images of an outlaw. Pages 12–13 in K. Springer, ed. *Biologue: A journal of interpretation and discovery in the life sciences*. Teton Science School, Kelly, Wyoming.

Edelman, P. 1990. *Critical wildlife corridor/habitat linkage areas between the Santa Susanna Mountains, the Simi Hills and the Santa Monica Mountains*. Prepared for the Nature Conservancy. The Santa Monica Mountains Conservancy. Malibu, California.

Errington, P.L. 1967. *Of predation and life*. Iowa State University Press, Ames.

Evans, W. 1983. *The cougar in New Mexico: Biology, status, depredation of livestock, and management recommendations*. New Mexico Department of Fish and Game, Santa Fe.

Ewer, R.F. 1973. *The carnivores*. Cornell University Press, New York. (Cited from Kitchener 1991.)

Farnsworth, C.L. 1980. A descriptive analysis of the extent of commercial poaching in the United States. Ph.D. dissertation, Sam Houston State University, Huntsville, Texas.

Fergus, C. 1991. The Florida panther Verges on Extinction. *Science* 251:1178–1180.

Gabbert, A., and F.R. Henderson. 1990. *Puma in Kansas*. Cooperative Extension Service. Kansas State University. Manhattan, Kansas. July 1990.

Garnass, S., and M. Robinson. 1991. Lion suspected in jogger death. *The Denver Post*, 17 January 1991.

Glick, D. 1990. The new killing fields. *Newsweek* (July 23, 1990): 54–55.

Green, J.S. 1981. Reducing coyote damage to sheep with nonlethal techniques. *Proceedings of the fifth Great Plains wildlife damage control workshop*, Lincoln, Nebraska.

Grey, Z. 1922. *Tales of the lonely trails*. Blue Ribbon Books, New York. (Cited from Acuff 1988.)

Guggisberg, C.A.W. 1975. *Wild cats of the world*. Taplinger Publishing Co., New York.

Halfpenny, J., and E. Biesiot. 1986. *A field guide to mammal tracking in North America*. Johnson Books, Boulder, Colorado.

Hall, E.R. 1981. *The mammals of North America*. 2nd ed. John Wiley and Sons, New York. 2 vols. (Cited from Kitchener 1991.)

Harpster, J. 1990. Floridians fight to save panthers. *The Christian Science Monitor*, 24 April 1990.

Harrington, J.P. 1916. Ethnogeography of the Tewa Indians, *Bureau of American Ethnology annual report*, vol. 29 (1916), pp. 29– 636. Washington, D.C. (Cited from Acuff 1988.)

Harris, L.D. 1985. Conservation corridors: A highway system for wildlife. *ENFO*, November.

————, and P.B. Gallagher. 1989. New initiatives for wildlife conservation: The need for movement corridors. Pages 11–34 *in* Gay Mackintosh, ed. *Preserving communities and corridors.* Defenders of Wildlife, Washington, D.C.

Hebert, D. 1989. The status and management of cougar in British Columbia 1988. Pages 11–14 *in* R.H. Smith, ed. *Proceedings of the third mountain lion workshop,* Prescott, Arizona.

Hemker, T.P. 1982. Population characteristics and movement patterns of cougars in southern Utah. M.S. thesis, Utah State University, Logan.

————., F.G. Lindzey, and B.B. Ackerman. 1984. Population characteristics and movement patterns of cougars in southern Utah. *Journal of Wildlife Management* 48(4):1275–1284.

————., F.G. Lindzey, B.B. Ackerman, and A.J. Button. 1986. Survival of cougar cubs in a nonhunted population. Page 327–332 *in* S.D. Miller and D.D. Everett, eds. *Cats of the world: Biology, conservation and management.* Proceedings of the Second International Cat Symposium. Caesare Kleberg Wildlife Research Institute. Kingsville, Texas.

Hibben, F.C. 1937. *A preliminary study of the mountain lion* (Felis oregonensis [sub] sp.). The University of New Mexico Bulletin. Biological Series 5(3):1–59.

Hill, E.G. 1991. *A review of the Department of Fish and Game: Issues and options for improving its performance.* Legislative Analyst's Office. Sacramento, California. September 3, 1991.

Hodge, G.M. 1967. *The kachinas are coming: Pueblo Indian kachina dolls with related folk tales.* Northland Publishing, Flagstaff, Arizona. (Cited from Acuff 1988.)

Hopkins, R.A. 1989. Ecology of the puma in the Diablo Range, California. Ph.D. dissertation, University of California at Berkeley.

Horan, A. 1992a. 6 cougars were hit on OC roads in '91, study says. *The Orange County Register,* 24 January 1992.

————. 1992b. Adults only park rule draws criticism. *The Orange County Register,* 7 February 1992.

Hornocker, M.G. 1969a. Winter territoriality in mountain lions. *Journal of Wildlife Management* 33:457–464.

————. 1969b. Stalking the mountain lion—to save him. *National Geographic* (November): 638–655.

————. 1970. An analysis of mountain lion predation upon mule deer and elk in the Idaho Primitive Area. *Wildlife Monographs* 21:1–39.

————., C. Jonkel, and L.D. Mech. 1979. Family felidae. Mountain lion (*Felis concolor*). *Wild animals of North America.* National Geographic, Washington, D.C.

————, and G.M. Koehler. 1985. Reintroducing orphaned mountain lion kittens into the wild. Pages 167–169 *in* J. Roberson and F. Lindzey, eds. *Proceedings of the second mountain lion workshop,* Salt Lake City.

Houston, A., C. Clark, J. McNamara, and M. Mangel. 1988. Dynamic models in behavioral and evolutionary ecology. *Nature* 332:29–34. (Cited from Kitchener 1991.)

Hummel, M. 1990. *A conservation strategy for large carnivores in Canada.* World Wildlife Fund Canada, Toronto.

Jordan, D. 1990a. Mercury contamination: Another threat to the Florida panther. *Endangered Species Technical Bulletin* 15(2). Department of the Interior, U.S. Fish and Wildlife Service, Washington, D.C.

————. 1990b. *Final environmental assessment: A proposal to issue endangered species permits to capture select Florida panthers and establish a captive population.* U.S. Fish and Wildlife Service. Gainsville, Florida.

Johnson, T.B. 1990. Yuma puma. *Wildlife Views.* Arizona Game and Fish Department. Phoenix, Arizona. August.

Kellert, S.R. 1979. *Public attitudes toward critical wildlife and natural habitat issues.* U.S. Government Printing Office #024-010-00-623-4, Washington, D.C. (Cited from Kellert 1985.)

———. 1980. *Activities of the American public relating to animals.* U.S. Government Printing Office # 024-010-00-624-2, Washington, D.C.

———., and J.K. Berry. 1981. *Knowledge, affection and basic attitudes toward animals in American society.* U.S. Government Printing Office #024-010-00-625-1, Washington, D.C. (Cited from Kellert 1985.)

———. 1985. Birdwatching in American society. *Leisure Sciences* 7(3):343–360.

Kiltie, R.A. 1991. How cats work. Pages 54–67 *in* J. Seidensticker and S. Lumpkin, eds. *Great cats: Majestic creatures of the wild.* Rodale Press, Emmaus, Pennsylvania.

Kiplinger Washington Editors. 1985. *1985 Kiplinger forecast of Florida's growth during the next ten years–by localities.* The Kiplinger Washington Editors, Inc. Washington, D.C.

Kitchener, A. 1991. *The natural history of the wild cats.* Cornell University Press. Ithaca, New York.

Koehler, G.M., and M.G. Hornocker. 1985. Mountain lions as a mortality factor in bobcats. Pages 170–171 *in* J. Roberson and F. Lindzey, eds. *Proceedings of the second mountain lion workshop,* Salt Lake City.

Laing, S.P. 1988. Cougar habitat selection and spatial use patterns in southern Utah. M.S. thesis. University of Wyoming, Laramie.

Lait, M. 1991. $2 million awarded to girl mauled by mountain lion. *Los Angeles Times,* 24 August 1991.

Lange, C.H. 1959. *Cochiti: A New Mexican pueblo past and present.* University of Texas Press, Austin. (Cited from Acuff 1988.)

Laycock, G. 1988. Cougars in conflict. *Audubon* (March): 86–95.

Leopold, A. 1933. *Game management.* The University of Wisconsin Press, Madison, Wisconsin.

———. 1949. *A sand county almanac.* Oxford University Press, London.

Leopold, B.D., and P.R. Krausman. 1986. Diets of 3 predators in Big Bend National Park, Texas. *Journal of Wildlife Management* 50(2):290–295.

Leyhausen, P. 1979. *Cat behavior: The predatory and social behavior of domestic and wild cats.* Garland STPM Press, New York. Translated by B.A. Tomkin.

Lindzey, F. 1987. Mountain lion. Pages 656–668 *in* M. Novak, J.A. Baker, M.E. Obbard, and B. Malloch, eds. *Wild furbearer management and conservation in North America.* Ministry of Natural Resources, Ontario, Canada.

———., B.B. Ackerman, D. Barnhurst, and T.P. Hemker. 1988. Survival rates of mountain lions in southern Utah. *Journal of Wildlife Management* 52:664–667.

———., B.B. Ackerman, D. Barnhurst, T. Becker, T.P. Hemker, S.P. Laing, C. Mecham, and W.D. Van Sickle. 1989. *Boulder-Escalante cougar project final report.* Utah Division of Wildlife Resources, Salt Lake City, Utah.

———., W.D. Van Sickle, S.P. Laing, and C.S. Mecham. 1992. Simulated cougar harvest in southern Utah. *Journal of Wildlife Management.* In Press.

Loftis, R.L. 1991. Protection for mountain lions sought: Sierra Club wants killings limited. *The Dallas Morning News,* 12 December 1991.

Logan, K.A. 1983. Mountain lion population and habitat characteristics in the Big Horn Mountains of Wyoming. M.S. thesis, University of Wyoming, Laramie.

———, and L.L. Irwin. 1985. Mountain lion habitats in the Big Horn Mountains, Wyoming. *Wildlife Society Bulletin* 13:257–262.

Lopez, B. 1981. The elusive mountain lion. *GEO* (June): 98–116.

Lowery, G.H. Jr. 1936. A preliminary report on the distribution of the mammals of Louisiana. *Proceedings of the Louisiana Academy of Sciences* 3:11–39. (Cited from Belden 1989.)

Lynch, W. 1989. The elusive cougar. *Canadian Geographic* (August/ September): 24–31.

Macgregor, W.G. 1976. The status of the puma in California. Pages 28–35 *in* R.L. Eaton, ed. *The world's cats, vol. 3(1): Contributions to status, management and conservation.* Carnivore Research Institute, University of Washington, Seattle. (Cited from Dixon 1982.)

Maehr, D.S., J.C. Roof, E.D. Land, and J.W. McCown. 1989. First reproduction of a panther *(Felis concolor coryi)* in southwestern Florida. *Mammalia* 53:129–131

———. 1990a. The Florida panther and private lands. *Conservation Biology* 4(2):167–170.

———. 1990b. Tracking Florida's panthers. *Defenders* (September/ October):10–15.

———., E.D. Land, J.C. Roof, and J.W. McCown. 1990c. Day beds, natal dens, and activity of Florida panthers. *Proceedings of the Annual Conference of Southeast Fish and Wildlife Agencies,* 44: In Press.

———., R.C. Belden, E.D. Land, and L. Wilkins. 1990d. Food habits of panthers in southwest Florida. *Journal of Wildlife Management* 54(3):420–423.

———., E.D. Land, and J.C. Roof. 1991a. Social ecology of Florida panthers. *National Geographic Research & Exploration* 7(4):414–431.

———., E.D. Land, and M.E. Roelke. 1991b. Mortality patterns of panthers in southwest Florida. *Proceedings of the annual conference of southeast fish and wildlife agencies* 45:In press.

Mansfield, T.M., and R.A. Weaver. 1989. The status of mountain lions in California. Pages 15–18 *in* R.H. Smith, ed. *Proceedings of the third mountain lion workshop,* Prescott, Arizona.

McMahan, L.R. 1982. The international cat trade. Pages 461–488 *in* S.D. Miller and D.D. Everett (eds.). *Cats of the world: Biology, conservation and management.* Proceedings of the Second International Cat Symposium. Caesare Kleberg Wildlife Research Institute. Kingsville, Texas.

McMullen, J.P. 1984. *Cry of the panther: Quest of a species.* Pineapple Press, Englewood, Florida.

McTaggert-Cowan, Ian. 1989. Room at the top? from *Endangered Spaces,* Monte Hummel, Gen. Ed. Key Porter Books, Toronto, Ontario. (Cited from Hummel 1990.)

Melcher, J. 1987. Cougars: Anatomy of a kill. Pages 7–9 *in* K. Springer, ed. *Biologue: A journal of interpretation and discovery in the life sciences.* Teton Science School, Kelly, Wyoming.

Mellen, J. 1991. Cat behavior. Pages 68–75 *in* J. Seidensticker and S. Lumpkin, eds. *Great cats: Majestic creatures of the wild.* Rodale Press, Emmaus, Pennsylvania.

Mills, E. 1922. *Watched by wild animals.* New York: Doubleday. (Cited From Acuff 1988.)

Mills, J. 1990. Deer old game. *National Wildlife* (October–November 1990):5–9.

Milstein, M. 1989. The quiet kill. *National Parks* (May/June 1989):19–24.

Montijo, Y. 1990. The story of the mountain lion. *News From Native California* (Spring 1990): 56.

Moreno, E.M. 1991. 'Big-cat' case jury convicts couple. *The Monterey Herald,* 26 June 1991.

Morse, S.C. 1989. Begging the question: What is mountain lion management? Pages 3–4 *in* R.H. Smith, ed. *Proceedings of the third mountain lion workshop,* Prescott, Arizona.

Mountain lion felled by hunter. 1991. *Denver Post,* 17 November 1991.

Murphy, K. 1983. *Characteristics of a hunted population of mountain lions in western Montana. (Relationships between a mountain lion population and hunting pressure in western Montana.)* Report to the Montana Department of Fish, Wildlife and Parks.

Neff, N.A. 1991. The cats and how they came to be. Pages 14–23 *in* J. Seidensticker and S. Lumpkin, eds. *Great cats: Majestic creatures of the wild.* Rodale Press. Emmaus, Pennsylvania,

Nero, R.W., and R.E. Wrigley. 1977. Status and habits of the cougar in Manitoba. *The Canadian Field-Naturalist* 91:28–40.

Newcomb, F.J. 1965. Origin of the Navajo Eagle Chant. In *Journal of American Folklore,* vol. 53 (1965), pp. 50–77. (Cited from Acuff 1988.)

Newmark, W.D. 1986. Species-area relationship and its determinants for mammals in western North American national parks. *Biological Journal of the Linnean Society* 28: 83–98.

Nowak, R.M. 1976. *The cougar in the United States and Canada.* New York Zoological Society and U.S. Fish and Wildlife Service Office of Endangered Species, Washington, D.C.

O'Brien, S.J., M.E. Roelke, N. Yuhki, K.W. Richards, W.E. Johnson, W. L. Franklin, A.E. Anderson, O.L. Bass Jr., R.C. Belden, and J.S. Martenson. 1990. Genetic introgression within the Florida panther *Felis concolor coryi. National Geographic Research* 6(4):485–494.

———. 1991. Molecular evolution of cats. Page 18 *in* J. Seidensticker and S. Lumpkin, eds. *Great cats: Majestic creatures of the wild.* Rodale Press. Emmaus, Pennsylvania.

———, and Mayr E. 1991. Bureaucratic mischief: Recognizing endangered species and subspecies. *Science* 251:1187–1188.

Pall, O., M. Jalkotzy, and I. Ross. 1988. *The cougar in Alberta.* Fish and Wildlife Division. Alberta Forestry, Lands and Wildlife. Associated Resource Consultants. Calgary, Alberta.

Palmer, T. 1991. The final act? *Buzzworm: The Environmental Journal* (November/December):31–35.

Parfit, M. 1985. Its days as a varmint are over, but the cougar is still on the run. *Smithsonian* (November): 68–79.

Parker, G. 1983. The eastern cougar in the Maritime provinces. *New Brunswick Naturalist* 12(4):151–155.

Parsons, E.C. 1936. *Taos Pueblo.* Banta Publishing Co., Menasha, Wisconsin (Cited from Acuff 1988.)

———. 1939. *Pueblo Indian religion.* University of Chicago Press, Chicago. (Cited from Acuff 1988.)

Phelps, J.S. 1989. Status of mountain lions in Arizona. Pages 7–9 *in* R.H. Smith, ed. *Proceedings of the third mountain lion workshop,* Prescott, Arizona.

Poten, C.J. 1991. A shameful harvest: America's illegal wildlife trade. *National Geographic* (September 1991).

Predator control: Death as a way of life. 1971. *Environmental Action,* 21 August 1971.

Quigley, H. 1990. The complete cougar. *Wildlife Conservation* (March/April): 67.

Rabb, G.G. 1959. Reproductive and vocal behavior in captive pumas. *Journal of Mammalogy* 49:616–617. (Cited from Dixon 1982.)

Reisner, M. 1987. Bad news, bears. *California Magazine* (March): 71–128

Rember, J. 1990. Cougar: The all-American predator. *Wildlife Conservation* (March/April): 60–79.

Roberts, R. 1990. There is no turning back: Instincts of deer lead them across roads, where they lose escape skills. *Los Angeles Times,* 31 October 1990.

Robertson, W.B., Jr., O.L. Bass J., and R.T. McBride. 1985. *Review of existing information of the Florida panther in the Everglades National Park, Big Cypress National Preserve and Environs with suggestions for need and research.* Everglades National Park. Homestead, Florida. (Cited from Belden 1989.)

Robinette, W.L., J.S. Gashwiler, and O.W. Morris. 1959. Food habits of the cougar in Utah and Nevada. *Journal of Wildlife Management* 23:261–273.

———. 1961. Notes on cougar productivity and life history. *Journal of Mammalogy* 42:204–217.

Roelke, M.E. 1987. *Florida panther biomedical investigation. Annual performance report*. Endangered Species Project E-1-11. Florida Game and Fresh Water Fish Commission. (Cited from Belden 1989.)

Rozek, M. 1989. The man who saved america's lion. *Ford Times* (September): 34–39.

Russ, W.B. 1989. Status of the mountain lion in Texas. Pages 30–31 in R.H. Smith, ed. *Proceedings of the third mountain lion workshop,* Prescott, Arizona.

Sacks, J.J., R.W. Satin, and S.E. Bonzo. 1989. Dog bite fatalities from 1979 through 1988. *Journal of the American Medical Association* 262:1489–1492. (Cited from Beier 1991.)

Saxton, D.F., and L. Saxton. 1973. *O'othham Hoho'ok A'githa: Legends and lore of the Papago and Pima Indians*. University of Arizona Press, Tucson. (Cited from Acuff 1988.)

Satchell, M., and J.M. Schorf. 1990. Uncle Sam's war on wildlife. *U.S. News and World Report* (February 5): 36–37.

Schneider, K. 1991. Big federal hunts of predators may backfire, biologists warn. *The Sacramento Bee,* 9 June 1991.

Schrader, E. 1991. Big-game hunting organizers convicted. *San Jose Mercury News,* 26 June 1991.

Schueler, D.G. 1980. *Incident at Eagle Ranch: Man and predator in the American West*. Sierra Club Books. San Francisco, California.

Seal, U.S., R.C. Lacy, and workshop participants. 1989. *Florida panther viability analysis and species survival plan*. Captive Breeding Specialist Group, Species Survival Commission, IUCN. Gainsville, Florida.

Seidensticker, J.C., IV, 1991a. Pumas. Pages 130–138 in J. Seidensticker and S. Lumpkin, eds. *Great cats: Majestic creatures of the wild*. Rodale Press. Emmaus, Pennsylvania.

———. 1991b. Introduction to The living cats by F.C. Sunquist. Page 28 in J. Seidensticker and S. Lumpkin, eds. *Great cats: Majestic creatures of the wild*. Rodale Press. Emmaus, Pennsylvania.

———, and S. Lumpkin. 1992. Mountain lions don't stalk people. True or false? *Smithsonian* (February):113–122.

———, M.G. Hornocker, W.V. Wiles, and J.P. Messick. 1973. Mountain lion social organization in the Idaho Primitive Area. *Wildlife Monographs,* 35.

Shaw, H. 1987. *Mountain lion field guide*. 3rd Edition. Special Report Number 9. Arizona Game and Fish Department.

———. 1989. *Soul among lions*. Johnson Books. Boulder, Colorado.

Shorma, G. 1989. Status of the mountain lion in Wyoming. Pages 38–39 in R.H. Smith, ed. *Proceedings of the third mountain lion workshop,* Prescott, Arizona.

Sibbison, H.R. 1984. So sheep may safely graze. *Defenders:*11–19.

Sitton, L.W., and S. Wallen. 1976. *California mountain lion study*. California Department of Fish and Game. Sacramento.

———, and R.A. Weaver. 1977. *California mountain lion investigations with recommendations for management*. California Department of Fish and Game, Sacramento.

Spalding, D.J., and J. Lesowski. 1971. Winter food of the cougar in south central British Columbia. *Journal of Wildlife Management* 35:378–381.

Smith, R.H., ed. 1989. *Proceedings of the third mountain lion workshop*. Prescott, Arizona.

Spargo, J. 1950. *The catamount in Vermont*. Bennington, Vermont.

Stegner, W. 1981. *Memo to the mountain lion.* Written exclusively for Operation Wildlife. Mountain Lion Foundation. Sacramento, California.

Steinhardt, P. 1989. Taming our fear of predators. *National Wildlife* (February/March): 4–12.

Stiver, S.J. 1989. Status of mountain lions in Nevada. Pages 26–29 *in* R.H. Smith, ed. *Proceedings of the third mountain lion workshop,* Prescott, Arizona.

Storer, T.I. 1923. Rabies in a mountain lion. *California Fish and Game* April 9(2):45–48.

Streubel, D. 1990. Mountain lion under study in Idaho. *Northern Rockies Conservation Cooperative News* (Summer): 8.

Suminski, H.R. 1982. Mountain lion predation on domestic livestock in Nevada. *Proceedings of the vertebrate pest conference* 10:62–66.

Sunquist, F.C. 1987. The nature of cats. Pages 19–29 *in Kingdom of cats.* National Wildlife Federation. Washington D.C.

———. 1991. The living cats. Pages 28–53 *in* J. Seidensticker and S. Lumpkin, eds. *Great cats: Majestic creatures of the wild.* Rodale Press, Emmaus, Pennsylvania.

Sward, S. 1990. Endangered Species Act's successes have been few. *San Francisco Chronicle,* 14 May 1990.

Sweanor, L.L. 1990. Mountain lion social organization in a desert environment. M.S. thesis, University of Idaho, Moscow.

Swendsen, D.H. 1985. *Badge in the wilderness: My 30 dangerous years combating wildlife violaters.* Stackpole Books, Harrisburg, Pennsylvania.

Thornback, J., and M. Jenkins, eds. 1982. *The IUCN Mammal Red Data Book,* Part 1. IUCN, Gland, Switzerland.

Tinsley, J.B. 1970. *The Florida panther.* Great Outdoors Publishing. St. Petersburg, Florida. (Cited from Belden 1989.)

———. 1987. *The puma: Legendary lion of the Americas.* Texas Western Press, The University of Texas at El Paso.

Trulio, L. 1989a. *Livestock depredation: Why lions are not a major threat to California's livestock industry.* Pouncing on the myths about mountain lions, volume IV, Mountain Lion Preservation Foundation Series, Sacramento, California.

———. 1989b. *What mountain lion scientists say about their research: Results of a survey on mountain lion research methods.* Mountain Lion Preservation Foundation, Sacramento, California.

Tully, R.J. 1991. *Summary of 1991 questionnaire on mountain lion hunting regulations.* Mountain Lion-Human Interaction Symposium and Workshop, April 24–26, Denver, Colorado, Division of Wildlife.

Turbak, G., and A. Carey. 1986. *America's great cats.* Northland Publishing, Flagstaff, Arizona.

U.S. Department of Agriculture. 1990. Animal and Plant Health Inspection Service. *Animal damage control program, draft environmental impact statement-1990.*

U.S. Department of the Interior. 1982. *1980 National hunting, fishing and wildlife-related recreation survey.* Washington, D.C. (Cited from Kellert 1985.)

U.S. Department of the Interior/Fish and Wildlife Service. 1989. Endangered and threatened wildlife and plants; animal notice of review. *Federal Register,* January 6, 1989.

U.S. Fish and Wildlife Service. 1979. *Ranchers say electric fencing protects sheep from coyotes.* Denver Wildlife Research Center, Denver, Colorado.

———. 1987. *Florida panther recovery plan.* Technical Subcommittee of the Florida Panther Interagency Committee. June 1987.

———. 1991. *Endangered and threatened wildlife and plants, 50 CFR 17.11 & 17.12, July 15, 1991.* U.S. Government Printing Office: 1991-296-520:50024. Washington D.C.

Van Dyke, F.G., R.H. Brocke, H.G. Shaw, B.B. Ackerman, T.P. Hemker, and F.G. Lindzey. 1986. Reactions of mountain lions to logging and human activity. *Journal of Wildlife Management* 50(1):95–102.

Van Meter, V.B. 1988. *The Florida panther*. Florida Power & Light Company.

Van Valkenburgh, B. 1991. Cats in communities: Past and present. Page 16 *in* J. Seidensticker and S. Lumpkin, eds. *Great cats: Majestic creatures of the wild*. Rodale Press. Emmaus, Pennsylvania.

Wallace, J. 1986. Has the big cat come back? *Sierra* (May/June):20–21.

Wallmo, O.C. 1978. Mule and black-tailed deer. Pages 30–41 *in* J.L. Schmidt and D.L. Gilbert, eds. *Big game of North America: Ecology and management*. Wildlife Management Institute. Stackpole Books.

Walls, G.L. 1942. *The vertebrate eye*. Harper, New York. (Cited from Kitchener 1991.)

Weiss, R. 1990. Researchers foresee antivenin improvements. *Science News* 138:360–362. (Cited from Beier 1991.)

White, L.A. 1942. *The Pueblo of Santa Ana, New Mexico*. Memoirs of the American Anthropological Association, vol. 60. (Cited from Acuff 1988.)

Whitfield, P. 1978. *The hunters*. Simon and Schuster, New York.

Wild cougar captured in Worthington. 1991b. *Austin Herald, 23 December 1991.*

Wright, B. S. 1959. *The ghost of North America: The story of the eastern panther*. Vantage Press, New York.

———. 1972. *The eastern panther: A question of survival*. Clark Irwin, Toronto.

Yanez, J.L, J.C. Cardenas, P. Gezelle, and F.M. Jaksic. 1986. Food habits of the southernmost mountain lions (*Felis concolor*) in South America: Natural versus livestocked ranges. *Journal of Mammology* 67(3):604–606.

Young, S.P., and E.A. Goldman. 1946. *The puma: Mysterious American cat*. American Wildlife Institute, Washington, D.C.

·INDEX·